UNDERWRAPS!

The publisher wishes to thank **Parkson Grand Sdn. Bhd.** for the loan and use of their tableware.

Photographer: Rory Daniels
Designer: Lynn Chin Nyuk Ling
Editor: Sim Ee Waun

Published by Marshall Cavendish Cuisine
An imprint of Marshall Cavendish International
1 New Industrial Road, Singapore 536196

Other Marshall Cavendish Offices

Marshall Cavendish Ltd. 119 Wardour Street, London W1F OUW, UK • Marshall Cavendish Corporation. 99 White Plains Road, Tarrytown NY 10591-9001, USA • Marshall Cavendish International (Thailand) Co Ltd. 253 Asoke, 12th Flr, Sukhumvit 21 Road, Klongtoey Nua, Wattana, Bangkok 10110, Thailand • Marshall Cavendish (Malaysia) Sdn Bhd, Times Subang, Lot 46, Subang Hi-Tech Industrial Park, Batu Tiga, 40000 Shah Alam, Selangor Darul Ehsan, Malaysia

Marshall Cavendish is a trademark of Times Publishing Limited

National Library Board Singapore Cataloguing in Publication Data

Teoh, Debbie.
Under wraps! / Debbie Teoh. — Singapore : Marshall Cavendish Cuisine, c2005.
p. cm.
ISBN : 981-232-964-1

1. Stuffed foods (Cookery) 2. Cookery, International. I. Title.

TX836
641.8 -- dc21 SLS2005039731

Printed in Singapore by Tien Wah Press (Pte Ltd)

UNDERWRAPS!

Debbie Teoh

Marshall Cavendish
Cuisine

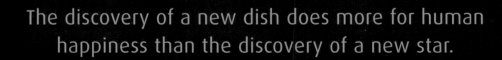

The discovery of a new dish does more for human happiness than the discovery of a new star.

~Jean Anthelme Brillat-Savarin

Dedication

I would like to dedicate this book to my dear mum, Madam Esther Teng, who turned 70 recently and who remains my pillar of strength. Thank you, mum, for everything.

Secondly, to the two steely ladies, Madam Annie Lim and Madam Tan Ah Nya, who helped me to discover and seal my passion for cooking and baking. Without them, I would not be here today.

To the photo shoot team—Rory, the photographer; Lynn, the food stylist and designer; and Selina, the editor—thanks for going through the bad haze and weather.

Lastly, to my family and friends who have supported me. You know who you are. There would not be enough space to list all your names! Thank you all from the bottom of my heart.

Contents

Preface

A wrapped parcel of food, much like a gift, has always been enticing. The mystery of its contents, the chance of a surprise and the excitement of uncovering are lures few can resist.

Under Wraps! aims to give a little something to everyone. The recipes in this book were inspired by many cultures, both Eastern and Western, and the diversity of flavours they encompass is marvellous and remarkable.

The culinary possibilities that follow from different types of wrappers, some edible and others not, are near infinite with some imagination—from coconut, banana and lotus leaves to phyllo pastry, spring roll skins, seaweed sheets and chapati.

I hope that my examples in this book will spur you to interpret and re-interpret the form that is the wrapper and the wrapped. Serve your loved ones endless 'gifts' and delight in their pleasure every time. Be happy, cook from your heart and the food should be nothing less than fabulous!

Meat and Poultry

Turmeric Leaves

Baked Chicken Char Siu Pau, Hong-Kong Style

INGREDIENTS

Egg	1, lightly beaten
Sesame seeds for garnishing	

Filling

Chicken fillet	400 g (13½ oz), cut into small cubes
Cooking oil	2 Tbsp
Garlic	1 clove, peeled and chopped
Sugar	50 g (2 oz) or to taste
Green peas	100 g (3½ oz)
Onions	2, large, peeled and cubed
Salt	½ tsp or to taste
Tapioca (cassava) flour	2 Tbsp, mixed with 2 Tbsp water
Sesame seeds	2 Tbsp

Seasoning

Oyster sauce	1 Tbsp
Dark soy sauce	1 tsp
Sesame oil	1 tsp
Chinese five-spice powder	1 tsp
Chicken stock granules	1 tsp

Water dough

Plain (all-purpose) flour	250 g (9 oz)
Baking powder	1 tsp
Castor (superfine) sugar	100 g (3½ oz)
Vegetable shortening	60 g (2 oz)
Lime (limau nipis) juice	1 Tbsp, or 1 tsp vinegar
Water	100 ml (3½ fl oz)

Oil dough

Plain (all-purpose) flour	250 g (9 oz)
Vegetable shortening	120 g (4 oz)
Salt	½ tsp

METHOD

- Prepare filling. Mix together chicken fillet and combined seasoning ingredients. Refrigerate for 20 minutes.
- Heat oil in a wok and sauté garlic until fragrant.
- Add chicken and sauté for 10 seconds, then add sugar, green peas and onions. Stir-fry to mix.
- Season to taste with salt and stir in tapioca flour solution to thicken. Turn off heat, sprinkle sesame seeds over and mix well. Set aside.
- Prepare water dough. Combine all ingredients, except water, in an electric mixer or mixing bowl. Gradually mix in sufficient water to form a smooth dough; you may not need all of the water. Leave to rest in the mixing bowl for 1 hour, covered with a clean tea towel.
- Prepare oil dough. Combine ingredients in an electric mixer or mixing bowl and blend until a soft dough forms. Divide into 30 equal portions.
- Divide rested water dough into 30 equal portions and roll out each portion into a round with a rolling pin.
- Place a ball of oil dough on top of a round of water dough. Gather up edges to enclose oil dough, seal and reshape into a ball.
- Flatten combined dough with a rolling pin into a round roughly 6 cm (2½ in) in diameter.
- Roll up the round Swiss-roll style, then flatten resulting log into a rectangle with a rolling pin.
- Roll up rectangle from the short side into a log. Place log on its side or make it stand vertically, then flatten into a round with a rolling pin.
- Place 1 rounded (heaped) tsp filling onto the centre of the round, gather edges above the filling and twist to seal.
- Place each prepared *pau* (bun) on a square sheet of baking paper, brush with beaten egg to glaze and sprinkle sesame seeds on top.
- Bake prepared *pau* in a preheated oven at 180°C (350°F) for 30 minutes or until golden brown. Serve warm.

Note: Char siu is a traditional Chinese dish of barbecued pork. In some parts of Asia, especially where there are significant Muslim populations, char siu is made from chicken. Ready-made chicken char siu or barbecued chicken, if available, may be used to save time. If doing so, replace 400 g chicken fillet with the same amount of chicken char siu and omit the seasoning ingredients.

Beef Negimaki with Asparagus

INGREDIENTS

Asparagus	40 thin stalks
Sugar	1 Tbsp
Cooking oil	1 Tbsp
Water for blanching	
Beef tenderloin (fillet)	250–300 g (9–10 oz), cut into 0.5-cm (¼-in) thick slices
Bamboo skewers or cocktail sticks	
Toasted sesame seeds for garnishing	

Sauce

Ground white pepper	to taste
Light soy sauce	125 ml (4 fl oz / ½ cup)
Sugar	2–3 Tbsp or to taste

METHOD

▎ Trim off and discard tough ends of cleaned asparagus. Each stalk should be about 9-cm (3½-in) long.

▎ Bring a medium saucepan of water to the boil. Add sugar and cooking oil.

▎ Add asparagus and blanch for about 20 seconds. The asparagus should be bright green and still crisp.

▎ Plunge blanched asparagus into a bowl of ice water to stop the cooking process. Drain and set aside.

▎ Combine all sauce ingredients in a small bowl and stir until sugar is dissolved.

▎ Pour one-third of the sauce into a separate container and set aside for use as a dipping sauce later.

▎ Trim beef slices into 5 x 3-cm (2 x 1½-in) rectangles or larger depending on the asparagus used. Pound meat slices lightly with the back of a knife.

▎ Dip beef into remaining sauce and place on a clean work surface. Place 1 or 2 asparagus stalks on top and roll to wrap beef around asparagus. Secure with a bamboo skewer or cocktail stick. Repeat until ingredients are used up.

▎ Pan- or oven-grill beef rolls at high heat for 1–2 minutes, basting with remaining sauce and turning over once. Remove when slightly charred.

▎ Sprinkle cooked rolls with sesame seeds. Serve hot with reserved dipping sauce or dipping sauce of choice, e.g. Thai sweet chilli sauce, for variation.

Note: Negimaki is a Japanese term for steak rolls. Traditionally, juicy slices of beef tenderloin were wrapped around spring onions (scallions) instead of asparagus tips.

Pot Stickers

Plain (all-purpose) flour	250 g (8³/₄ oz)
Hot water	125 ml (4 fl oz / ¹/₂ cup)
Tapioca (cassava) flour for dusting	

Filling

Chicken meat	125 g (4¹/₂ oz), chopped
Prawn (shrimp) meat	90 g (3 oz), chopped
Scallops	50 g (2 oz), chopped
Light soy sauce	1 Tbsp
Cooking oil	2 Tbsp and more for pan-frying
Sesame oil	1 tsp
Chicken stock granules	1 tsp
Spring onions (scallions)	20 g (³/₄ oz), sliced
Chinese chives (*ku cai*)	20 g (³/₄ oz), sliced
Ground white pepper	¹/₂ tsp or to taste
Salt	to taste

Vinegar dipping sauce

Black vinegar	3 Tbsp
Light soy sauce	1 Tbsp
Garlic	1 clove, peeled and chopped
Chopped coriander leaves (cilantro)	¹/₂ Tbsp
Sesame oil	1 tsp

METHOD

- Prepare filling. Combine chicken, prawn meat, scallops, light soy sauce, cooking oil, sesame oil and chicken stock granules in a bowl. Mix well.

- Add spring onions, chives and pepper. Season to taste with salt. Refrigerate until required.

- Prepare pot sticker skins. Combine plain flour and hot water in a mixing bowl. Mix using a spatula. When dough is cool enough to handle, knead until soft and pliable.

- Leave dough in the mixing bowl and cover with a damp tea towel. Set aside for 45 minutes to 1 hour for dough to rest.

- Meanwhile, prepare dipping sauce. Combine all ingredients in a small bowl and set aside until needed.

- To assemble, divide dough into 25 equal balls, then flatten and roll out into thin, 8-cm (3-in) rounds using a rolling pin.

- Place 1 rounded (heaped) tsp filling onto the centre of each round and fold in half to make a crescent-shaped dumpling. Tuck in left and right corners and press edges to seal.

- Heat sufficient cooking oil for pan-frying in a non-stick pan. Fry dumplings over medium to high heat for about 1 minute or until cooked. Dumplings should be golden brown at parts and crisp on all sides.

- Serve immediately with dipping sauce.

Note: **The name "pot stickers" is a literal translation of the Mandarin name for these dumplings—** *guo tie.*

Chicken in Pointed Pepper Leaves

Minced chicken	200 g (7 oz), or beef tenderloin
Tapioca (cassava) flour	1 Tbsp
Salt	to taste
Pointed pepper leaves (*daun kaduk*)	30–35
Bamboo skewers or cocktail sticks	
Cooking oil for brushing	

Marinade

Garlic	1 clove, peeled and sliced
Lemon grass (*serai*)	2 stalks, sliced
Shallots	2, peeled and sliced
Red chilli	1, sliced
Fish sauce	1 tsp
Honey	1 Tbsp
Cooking oil	1 Tbsp

Dipping sauce

Bird's eye chillies (*cili padi*)	3, thinly sliced
Garlic	2 cloves, peeled and chopped
Sugar	30 g (1 oz)
Lime (*limau nipis*) juice	3 Tbsp
Fish sauce	2 Tbsp
Water	80 ml (2$\frac{1}{2}$ fl oz)

METHOD

- Combine all dipping sauce ingredients in a bowl and season to taste. Set aside.

- Combine all marinade ingredients in a blender (processor) until fine. The liquid ingredients ensure that the blades will move well.

- In another bowl, mix together blended marinade and chicken. Add tapioca flour and salt to taste. Stir to blend, then refrigerate for 30 minutes.

- To assemble, spoon 1 tsp filling onto a pepper leaf, just below the centre and nearer the stem.

- Fold the stem end of the leaf over filling, then fold in left and right sides and roll up tightly; resulting log should be about 5-cm (2-in) long.

- Secure leaf roll with a bamboo skewer or cocktail stick. Trim off excess skewer or stick. Repeat until ingredients are used up.

- Brush rolls with oil and grill over moderately hot charcoal for 5–6 minutes or pan-fry for 2–3 minutes. Leaves will char slightly.

- Remove cooked rolls from heat and serve with dipping sauce.

Steamed Sago Beef Balls

Sago pearls — 250 g (9 oz), rinsed until water runs clear and drained in a colander before use

Boiling water — 100–120 ml (3½–4 fl oz)

Chinese lettuce leaves

Fresh coriander leaves (cilantro)

Filling

Cooking oil — 60 ml (2 fl oz / 4 Tbsp)

Shallots — 6, peeled and sliced

Garlic — 4 cloves, peeled and chopped

Ground coriander (*ketumbar serbuk*) — 1 Tbsp, mixed with 2 Tbsp water

Beef tenderloin (fillet) — 150 g (5 oz), minced

Castor (superfine) sugar — 50 g (2 oz)

Fish sauce — ½ Tbsp

Salt — ½ tsp or to taste

Skinned peanuts (groundnuts) — 100 g (3½ oz), roasted and finely ground

METHOD

▌ Prepare dough. Combine cleaned sago pearls and just enough boiling water to bind and form a dough.

▌ Divide dough into balls the size of limes (*limau nipis*), using some water for easier handling if necessary.

▌ Cover balls of dough with a clean, damp tea towel and set aside.

▌ Prepare filling. Heat oil in a pan and fry shallots until crisp. Remove and set aside.

▌ In the same oil, fry three-quarters of chopped garlic until light yellow and crisp. Drain and set aside.

▌ In still the same oil, fry remaining garlic and coriander paste until fragrant.

▌ Add minced beef and stir-fry until fragrant. Mix in sugar, fish sauce and salt to taste.

▌ Remove beef mixture from heat. Mix in ground peanuts and crisp-fried shallots.

▌ Divide filling into balls slightly smaller than dough balls.

▌ To assemble, flatten a ball of dough into a round and wrap a portion of filling with it, then seal and reshape into a ball. Repeat until ingredients are used up.

▌ Place prepared beef balls onto a greased tray and steam over high heat for 10 minutes.

▌ To serve, place a lettuce leaf on a plate and top with a few coriander leaves, then a steamed beef ball. Lastly, sprinkle on some crisp-fried garlic.

Note: The sago dough can become quite sticky. For easier handling, refrigerate the dough balls and the filling for 30 minutes before assembling.

Five-spice Chicken Rolls

Dried bean curd skin (*fu pei*)	2 large sheets, cut into 15 13 x 9-cm (5 x 3$\frac{1}{2}$-in) pieces
Plain (all-purpose) flour	2 Tbsp, mixed with 2 Tbsp water
Cooking oil for deep-frying	
Coriander leaves (cilantro) for garnishing	
Cucumbers (optional)	1, peeled if desired and sliced

Filling

Chicken fillet	500 g (1 lb 1$\frac{1}{2}$ oz), sliced
Yam (taro)	200 g (7 oz), peeled, cubed and steamed
Water chestnuts	5, peeled and sliced
Onion	1, large, peeled and sliced
Chinese five-spice powder	2 tsp
Oyster sauce	1 Tbsp
Tapioca (cassava) flour	2 rounded (heaped) Tbsp
Sesame oil	1 tsp
Sugar	2–3 Tbsp
Ground white pepper	$\frac{1}{2}$ tsp
Salt	$\frac{1}{2}$ tsp or to taste
Chicken stock granules	1 tsp

Dipping sauce

Thai sweet chilli sauce	75 ml (2$\frac{1}{2}$ fl oz / 5 Tbsp)
Peanut (groundnut) candy	2 Tbsp, coarsely ground
Lime (*limau nipis*) juice	extracted from 3 limes

METHOD

▋ Combine all the filling ingredients in a bowl and mix well. Refrigerate for 30 minutes.

▋ Combine all dipping sauce ingredients in a small bowl. Season to taste and set aside.

▋ Place 1 bean curd sheet on a clean work surface, with the short sides on your left and right.

▋ Spoon 2 Tbsp filling along the long side nearer to you, about 3 cm (1$\frac{1}{2}$ in) from the edge.

▋ Fold the lower edge over filling, then fold in left and right sides and roll up into a log.

▋ Seal with some flour paste. Repeat until ingredients are used up.

▋ Deep-fry prepared rolls in moderately hot oil for 3–5 minutes or until light brown and filling is cooked.

▋ Drain cooked rolls on absorbent paper towels.

▋ Serve rolls whole or cut into desired serving-size pieces. Garnish and serve with dipping sauce and freshly cut cucumber slices, if using.

Note: Traditional preparations of this recipe used pork instead of chicken. The dish is probably better known by its Hokkien name of *ngo hiang*, which literally translates into "five-spice".

Chicken Larb with Purple Cabbage

INGREDIENTS

Purple cabbage	1 head
Minced chicken	500 g (1 lb 1½ oz), preferably dark meat
Cooking oil	1 tsp
Salt	a pinch or more to taste
Water	60 ml (2 fl oz / 4 Tbsp)
Shallots	6, peeled and finely sliced
Lemon grass (serai)	4 stalks, finely sliced
Kaffir lime leaves (daun limau purut)	6, finely sliced
Bird's eye chillies (cili padi)	6, finely sliced
Lime (limau nipis) juice	extracted from 5–6 limes
Fish sauce	2 Tbsp
Sugar	4 tsp or to taste
Coriander leaves (cilantro) (optional)	30 g (1 oz), chopped

METHOD

▌ Separate cabbage into whole leaves. Wash and drain. Refrigerate until required.

▌ Season minced chicken meat with oil and salt.

▌ Combine chicken and water in a saucepan and cook until water is absorbed. Remove from heat.

▌ Transfer chicken to a mixing bowl and toss with remaining ingredients, except cabbage. Season to taste.

▌ Serve chicken mixture and cabbage leaves separately.

▌ Allow diners to spoon desired amounts of chicken mixture onto their cabbage leaves, then fold each leaf to enclose ingredients and eat out of hand.

Note: Larb gai is the name of a spicy and tangy minced chicken salad originating from northern Thailand.

Pandan Chicken

Chicken meat	600 g (1 lb 5 oz), thinly sliced, about 0.5-cm (1/4-in) thickness
Corn flour (cornstarch)	2–3 Tbsp
Fish sauce	2 Tbsp
Honey	90 ml (3 fl oz / 6 Tbsp) or to taste
Salt	2 tsp or to taste
Coconut milk	100 ml (3 1/2 fl oz)
Screwpine (*pandan*) leaves for wrapping	
Cooking oil for deep-frying	

Spice paste

Shallots	4, peeled
Garlic	3 cloves, peeled
Ginger	3-cm (1 1/2-in) knob, peeled
Lemon grass (*serai*)	3–4 stalks
Coriander (cilantro) root	1
Chilli powder (*cili serbuk*)	2 tsp
Ground turmeric (*kunyit serbuk*)	1 tsp
Cracked black peppercorns	1 tsp

METHOD

▌ Combine all spice paste ingredients in a blender (processor) until fine.

▌ Combine chicken slices, spice paste and remaining ingredients, except screwpine leaves and cooking oil, in a bowl. Mix well.

▌ Leave to marinate for at least 1 hour or preferably overnight in the refrigerator.

▌ To assemble, fold one end of screwpine leaf into a cone and fill with some marinated chicken.

▌ Fold down excess leaf to cover chicken, then wrap it around the back of the parcel, from left to right, and tuck it through the loop on the left to secure.

▌ The folding here is similar to that shown on pg 146 for *lepat kacang*, except that while pulling the excess leaf through the loop, adjust and shape parcel into a 2-pointed triangular shape.

▌ Deep-fry parcels in hot oil until cooked. The exposed chicken should be golden.

Note: Although *pandan* is the Malay name for screwpine leaves, this dish is Thai in origin.

Quail's Eggs Siu Mai

Shui kau (water dumpling)
  skins   30

Quail's eggs   30, hard-boiled and shelled

Crab roe or finely
  chopped carrot for
  garnishing

Filling

Prawn (shrimp) meat	150 g (5 oz), coarsely chopped
Chicken meat	100 g (3½ oz), minced
Fish paste	150 g (5 oz)
Egg white	1
Cooking oil	2 Tbsp
Corn flour (cornstarch)	1 Tbsp
Light soy sauce	1 tsp
Oyster sauce	1 tsp
Sesame oil	1 tsp
Chicken stock granules	1 tsp
Ground white pepper	½ tsp
Dried Chinese mushrooms	3, soaked to soften, stems discarded and cubed
Water chestnuts	5, peeled and chopped
Spring onions (scallions)	1, sliced
Salt	to taste

METHOD

▌ Prepare filling. Combine all ingredients, except mushrooms, water chestnuts and spring onions, in a bowl. Mix well.

▌ Add mushrooms, water chestnuts and spring onions, then season to taste. Refrigerate until needed.

▌ To assemble, place 1 Tbsp filling onto the centre of a dumpling skin and top with a quail's egg. Lift edges and smooth upwards until perpendicular; pleats will form on their own. Repeat until ingredients are used up.

▌ Place prepared *siu mai* (meat dumplings) on a greased tray and steam over rapidly boiling water for 8 minutes or until cooked.

▌ Serve warm and garnished, with dipping sauce of choice, if desired.

Note: Siu mai—steamed dumplings of minced pork and prawns—are a classic dim sum item. Here, they are prepared with chicken instead and the addition of quail's eggs not only is novel, but also adds great texture.

Steamed Herbal Chicken in Lotus Leaves

INGREDIENTS

Chicken	1, 1.2–1.4 kg (2 lb 10 oz–3 lb 2 oz), cleaned and preferably free range
Chinese rice wine	1 Tbsp
Salt	1 tsp
Ground white pepper	1 tsp
Aluminium foil	
Lotus leaves	2, large, pre-soaked
Dried chestnuts	10, cleaned and parboiled for 10 minutes

Herbal stock

Water	375 ml (12 fl oz / 1½ cups)
Codonopsis root (*dang shen/dong sum*)	30 g (1 oz)
Soloman's seal (*yu zhu/yoke chok*)	20 g (¾ oz)
Chinese angelica (*dang gui/tong kwai*)	15 g (½ oz)
Dried red dates (*hong zao/hung cho*)	12, pitted
Chinese wolfberries (*gou qi zi/kei chi*)	15 g (½ oz)

Seasoning

Cornflour (cornstarch)	2 Tbsp, mixed with 2 Tbsp water
Rock sugar	1 Tbsp or 10 g (⅓ oz)
Light soy sauce	1 Tbsp
Dark soy sauce	1 tsp
Chinese rice wine	2 Tbsp or to taste
Sesame oil	1 tsp
Oyster sauce	1 Tbsp
Ground white pepper	1 tsp
Salt	1 tsp or to taste
Chicken stock granules	1 tsp

METHOD

▌ Clean chicken thoroughly and pat dry with paper towels.

▌ Season chicken with Chinese wine, salt and pepper. Refrigerate for 30 minutes.

▌ Prepare herbal stock. Combine all ingredients in a pot and bring to the boil. Simmer for 5 minutes over medium to low heat.

▌ Remove stock from heat and stir in all seasoning ingredients. Leave to cool.

▌ Line a deep heatproof (flameproof) bowl large enough for the chicken and herbal stock with a large sheet of aluminium foil.

▌ Place 2 lotus leaves on top, then add chicken, cooled herbal stock and parboiled chestnuts.

▌ Wrap chicken and stock with lotus leaves into a parcel—fold in left and right sides, then fold up lower edge and fold down upper edge.

▌ Wrap lotus-leaf package with the foil to secure and prevent the stock from spilling out.

▌ Place foil parcel onto a steaming tray and steam over rapidly boiling water for 1 hour.

▌ Serve warm with steamed white rice or plain steamed Chinese dumplings.

Note: The Mandarin names of the Chinese herbs are given in Hanyu Pinyin on the left and on the right, are their names in transliterated Cantonese.

Fried Vietnamese Spring Rolls

Rice papers	24, softened with water before use
Cooking oil for deep-frying	
Chinese lettuce leaves	24, or salad leaves of choice
Fresh basil leaves	48
Mint leaves	48

Filling

Cooking oil	2 Tbsp
Garlic	2 cloves, peeled and chopped
Chicken fillet or beef	100 g (3$^{1}/_{2}$ oz), minced
Carrots	100 g (3$^{1}/_{2}$ oz), peeled if desired and julienned
Black (wood ear) fungus	10 g ($^{1}/_{3}$ oz), soaked and julienned
Chicken stock granules	1 tsp, mixed with 60 ml (2 fl oz / 4 Tbsp) water
French beans	50 g (2 oz), sliced
Transparent (glass) noodles (*tang hoon*)	100 g (3$^{1}/_{2}$ oz), blanched in hot water to soften and drained
Salt	$^{1}/_{2}$ tsp or to taste
Ground white pepper	$^{1}/_{2}$ tsp or to taste

Dipping sauce

Plum sauce	3 Tbsp
Orange juice and zest	from 1 orange
Fish sauce	1 Tbsp
Bird's eye chillies (*cili padi*)	3, sliced

METHOD

- Prepare filling. Heat oil in a pan and sauté garlic until fragrant.
- Add meat, carrots, black fungus and chicken stock. Simmer until chicken is cooked.
- Add French beans and transparent noodles. Stir to mix, then season to taste. Remove from heat and set aside.
- Prepare dipping sauce. Combine all ingredients in a bowl and season to taste. Set aside.
- Assemble spring rolls. Take 1 rounded (heaped) Tbsp filling and squeeze out any excess liquid, then spoon onto a sheet of rice paper; filling must be dry or else spring rolls will burst during frying.
- Fold in left and right sides and roll up tightly. Repeat until ingredients are used up.
- Heat sufficient oil for deep-frying in a wok over low–medium heat. Lower in rolls and cook until golden brown.
- Remove cooked rolls and place on paper towels to drain.
- To serve, place a lettuce leaf on a plate and top with 2 mint and 2 basil leaves. Put a fried spring roll on top, roll into a cylinder and serve with dipping sauce.

Roasted Loin of Lamb with Orange, Fig and Prune Dressing

INGREDIENTS

Lamb loin	1.4–1.6 kg (3 lb 2 oz–3 lb 9 oz)
Salt	to taste
Ground black pepper	to taste
Butter for basting	
Water or red wine	500 ml (16 fl oz / 2 cups)

Marinade

Extra virgin olive oil	60 ml (2 fl oz / 4 Tbsp)
Honey	60 ml (2 fl oz / 4 Tbsp)
Shallots	2, peeled and chopped
Cinnamon stick	1, 2.5-cm (1-in) long

Dressing

Dried figs	250 g (9 oz)
Dried prunes	250 g (9 oz), pitted
Water or red wine	3 Tbsp
Garlic	4 cloves, peeled and chopped
Fresh rosemary	2 Tbsp, finely chopped
Fresh thyme	2 Tbsp, finely chopped
Balsamic vinegar	2 Tbsp
Orange juice and zest	from 1 orange
Salt	1 tsp or to taste
Freshly ground black peppercorns	1 tsp or to taste

METHOD

▌ Marinate lamb with combined marinade ingredients and refrigerate overnight. The lamb should be covered with cling film (plastic wrap).

▌ Prepare dressing. Place figs, prunes and water or wine in a blender (processor) and pulse until they are coarsely chopped.

▌ Transfer blended ingredients to a bowl. Add garlic, rosemary, thyme, balsamic vinegar and orange zest and juice. Season to taste with salt and black pepper. Set aside.

▌ To assemble, cut marinated loin so that it opens like a book. Pound lightly with the back of a cleaver or a meat mallet to achieve an even thickness. Season with salt and black pepper.

▌ Spread half the dressing over the centre of loin, leaving a 2.5-cm (1-in) border all around. Reserve and refrigerate remaining dressing.

▌ Roll up loin and tie with kitchen twine or string at 2.5-cm (1-in) intervals. Wrap in cling film and refrigerate for 24 hours.

▌ Roast prepared loin in a preheated oven at 175°C (347°F) for 1 hour, basting occasionally with any pan drippings or butter.

▌ Rest loin for 10 minutes before serving.

▌ Meanwhile, prepare gravy. Combine water or wine with pan drippings and cook over low heat until liquid is reduced by half. Strain into a gravy boat.

▌ Warm up remaining dressing and serve together with lamb and gravy.

Note: **This fruity, festive dish requires two days of advanced preparation, but it is an impressive dish that makes the extra effort worthwhile.**

Beef Tenderloin in Corn Husks

INGREDIENTS

Beef tenderloin	700 g (1½ lb)
Ground black pepper	1 tsp
Cumin seeds (*jintan putih biji*)	1 tsp
Coriander seeds (*ketumbar biji*)	1 tsp
Ginger	2-cm (1-in) knob, peeled and chopped
Shallots	2, peeled and chopped
Garlic	1 clove, peeled and chopped
Olive oil	2 Tbsp
Salt	1 tsp
Dried corn husks	12, soaked in warm water for 1 hour, drained and pat dry
Olive oil for basting	

Mango Salsa

Pickled mango	200 g (7 oz), chopped
Bird's eye chillies (*cili padi*)	2–3, sliced
Tomatoes	1, about 100 g (3½ oz), chopped
Kalamansi lime (*limau kesturi*) juice and zest	from 5 limes
Sugar	50 g (2 oz)
Salt	1 tsp or to taste
Olive oil	1 Tbsp

METHOD

▌ Cut beef tenderloin into 10 rounds of about the same size, then pound lightly with the back of a cleaver. Set aside.

▌ Put black peppercorns, cumin and coriander into a small pan and stir over low heat for 1–2 minutes or until aromatic.

▌ Transfer dry-fried spices to a grinder and grind until fine.

▌ Combine ground spices, ginger, shallots, garlic, olive oil and salt in a small bowl and mix until a paste forms.

▌ Rub spice paste all over tenderloin pieces, then refrigerate, covered, for 1 hour.

▌ Meanwhile, prepare salsa. Combine all ingredients in a bowl and mix well, then refrigerate until needed.

▌ Prepare 20 strips of corn husk, each 1-cm (½-in) wide, by tearing up 2 corn husks; the strips will be used to tie the parcels later.

▌ Trim remaining corn husks, especially if large, into wrapping size; they should be able to enclose beef pieces completely.

▌ Wrap each piece of beef with corn husk, then tie each end with a strip. Ensure that beef is completely covered.

▌ Bake parcels in a preheated oven at 180°C (350°F) for 10–15 minutes or until cooked. Baste occasionally with olive oil. Alternatively, grill parcels over charcoal heat.

▌ Serve cooked beef topped with salsa.

Chicken Seaweed Rolls

Japanese seaweed (*nori*)	5 large sheets, cut into 10-cm (4-in) squares
Sesame seeds	100 g (3½ oz)
Cooking oil for deep-frying	

Filling

Chicken thigh meat	250 g (9 oz), finely minced
Water chestnuts	6, peeled and chopped
Prawn (shrimp) meat	100 g (3½ oz), chopped
Chopped young ginger	1 tsp
Egg	1
Cooking oil	1 Tbsp
Tapioca (cassava) flour	1 tsp
Chicken stock granules	1 tsp
Sesame oil	1 tsp
Ground white pepper	1 tsp
Salt	1 tsp or to taste

- Combine all filling ingredients in a bowl and mix well. Cover with cling film (plastic wrap). Refrigerate until needed.

- To assemble, spoon 1 Tbsp filling along the centre of a seaweed square. Roll up tightly and seal with some water.

- Coat both ends of the seaweed rolls with sesame seeds, then deep-fry over medium heat for 2 minutes or until cooked.

- Drain on paper towels, then serve immediately and as desired.

- One serving suggestion is to tie seaweed rolls into bundles of 3 with blanched spring onions (scallions).

Crystal Skin Dumplings

Cooking oil	2 Tbsp
Garlic	2 cloves, peeled and chopped
Dried prawns (shrimps)	50 g (2 oz), soaked and roughly chopped
Chicken fillet	80 g (3 oz), chopped
Yam bean (*bangkuang*)	100 g (3 1/2 oz), peeled and shredded
Carrot	50 g (2 oz), peeled if desired and finely chopped
Dried shiitake mushrooms	4, soaked to soften, stems discarded and julienned
Oyster sauce	1 Tbsp
Ground white pepper	1/4 tsp or to taste
Sugar	1 Tbsp or to taste
Salt	1 tsp or to taste
Cooking oil for brushing	

Crystal Skin

Wheat starch (*tang meen fun*)	80 g (3 oz)
Tapioca (cassava) flour	80 g (3 oz)
Cooking oil	2 Tbsp
Salt	1/2 tsp
Hot water	100 ml (3 1/2 fl oz)

METHOD

▌ Prepare filling. Heat oil in a wok over medium heat. Sauté garlic and dried prawns until light brown and fragrant.

▌ Add chicken, yam bean, carrot and mushrooms. Stir-fry for 1 minute or until vegetables are cooked.

▌ Season to taste with oyster sauce, pepper, sugar and salt. Remove from heat and set aside to cool.

▌ Prepare crystal skin. Combine wheat starch, tapioca flour, oil and salt in a mixing bowl.

▌ Using an electric beater fitted with a dough hook attachment, beat at low speed, adding hot water gradually until a smooth and pliable dough forms; you may not need all of the water.

▌ When ready to assemble, roll out dough into a thin layer with a rolling pin, then cut into 7-cm (3-in) rounds with a pastry cutter.

▌ Place 1 Tbsp filling onto the centre of each dough round. Fold dough skin in half, then pleat edges of one half onto the other half. Press lightly to seal.

▌ Repeat until ingredients are used up.

▌ Place prepared dumplings on a greased tray and steam over rapidly boiling water for 7 minutes or until cooked.

▌ Remove from steamer and brush with cooking oil. Serve warm.

Rolled Chapati with Chicken

Garlic	2 cloves, peeled
Ginger	1.5-cm ($^3/_4$-in) knob, peeled
Chilli powder (*cili serbuk*)	1 tsp or to taste
Garam masala	1 tsp, see note
Salt	1 tsp
Sugar	1 tsp
Yoghurt	1 Tbsp
Chicken thigh fillet	300 g (10 oz)
Cooking oil for basting	
Cream cheese	100 g ($3^1/_2$ oz)
Store-bought chapati	3, quartered
Chinese lettuce	2 bunches or to taste
Cucumber	1, cored and sliced into 5-cm (2-in) long strips
Onions	1, large, peeled and sliced
Spring onions (scallions)	2, leaves separated and scalded to soften

Dip

Yoghurt	125 ml (4 fl oz / $^1/_2$ cup)
Mint leaves	$^1/_2$ cup (15–20 g)

Garam masala (optional)

Cinnamon stick	3-cm ($1^1/_2$-in) long, broken into smaller pieces
Cardamoms	15 g ($^1/_2$ oz)
Cloves	$1^1/_2$ tsp
Cumin seeds (*jintan putih biji*)	$1^1/_2$ tsp
Black peppercorns	$1^1/_2$ tsp
Nutmeg	1, chopped into smaller pieces
Dried bay leaves	6, about 5 g ($^1/_6$ oz)

METHOD

▍ Pound garlic and ginger together until fine using a mortar and pestle.

▍ Combine pounded garlic and ginger with chilli powder, garam masala, salt, sugar and yoghurt. Mix in chicken and refrigerate for 1 hour to marinate.

▍ Oven-grill or bake chicken in a preheated oven at 220°C (440°F) for about 15 minutes or until browned. Baste chicken with some oil and turn over once.

▍ When done, remove chicken from oven and slice meat into long strips.

▍ To assemble, spread some cheese onto each chapati quarter, then top with a lettuce leaf, a length of cucumber, some onion slices and a strip of cooked chicken.

▍ Roll up into a cylindrical shape and tie with a length of softened spring onion. Repeat until ingredients are used up.

▍ Prepare dip. Blend (process) yoghurt and mint leaves until well combined, then transfer to a serving bowl. Serve immediately with chapati rolls.

▍ The mint-and-yoghurt dip should always be prepared last because the chopped mint discolours if allowed to sit.

Note: Garam masala is a north Indian spice mix that includes pepper, cumin, cardamom and cloves. It can be bought ready-made. To make your own, roast all ingredients in a pan over low heat for 15–20 seconds or until aromatic, then leave to cool thoroughly before grinding until fine. Store unused portion in an airtight jar.

Seafood

Screwpine Leaves

Grilled Fish with Mango and Cencaluk Sauce

INGREDIENTS

Scad (*ikan selar*) or chubb
  mackerel (*ikan kembung*)   2, cleaned and left whole, or
                     600 g (1 lb 5 oz) stingray
                     (*ikan pari*)

Banana leaves for wrapping

Cooking oil for basting

Seasoning

Ground turmeric (*kunyit serbuk*)	2 tsp
Chilli powder (*cili serbuk*)	2 tsp
Salt	1 tsp

Mango-cencaluk sauce

Fresh mango	1, semi-ripe, peeled and shredded, about 200 g (7 oz)
Bird's eye chillies (*cili padi*)	7–8, sliced
Shallots	5, peeled and sliced
Lime (*limau nipis*) juice	extracted from 3–4 limes
Preserved prawns (shrimps) (*cencaluk*)	60 ml (2 fl oz / 4 Tbsp)
Sugar	1 Tbsp

METHOD

▌ Rub fish with combined seasoning ingredients and refrigerate for 30 minutes to marinate.

▌ Combine all sauce ingredients in a mixing bowl and set aside until needed.

▌ Wrap marinated fish in banana leaves and grill over charcoal heat until cooked, takes 8–10 minutes depending on the size of fish. Baste with oil and turn over occasionally.

▌ Alternatively, pan-fry wrapped fish in 2 Tbsp oil until cooked.

▌ Serve cooked fish with the mango-*cencaluk* sauce.

Note: Cencaluk **is a pungent condiment made from fermented prawns (shrimps). It is especially popular among the Peranakan or Straits Chinese cooks from Penang in northern Malaysia.**

Grilled Otak-otak in Coconut Leaves

Prawn (shrimp) meat	200 g (7 oz)
Spanish mackerel (*ikan tenggiri*) meat	200 g (7 oz)
Turmeric leaf (*daun kunyit*)	1, finely sliced
Sugar	1 tsp or to taste
Salt	1½ tsp or to taste
Coconut leaves	50, each 20-cm (8-in) long and cleaned
Bamboo skewers or cocktail sticks	
Cooking oil for basting	

Rempah

Fresh red chilli	1, sliced
Dried chillies	5, about 8 g (¼ oz) dry weight, soaked and snipped into 2.5-cm (1-in) lengths
Lemon grass (*serai*)	3 stalks, sliced
Turmeric (*kunyit*)	5-cm (2-in) knob, about 20 g (¾ oz), peeled
Coriander seeds (*ketumbar biji*)	1 Tbsp
Cumin seeds (*jintan putih biji*)	1 Tbsp
Shallots	4, peeled and sliced
Dried prawn (shrimp) paste (*belacan*)	1 tsp, toasted
Coconut cream	125 ml (4 fl oz / ½ cup)

▌ Prepare *rempah*. Combine all ingredients using a blender (processor) until a fine paste forms. Set aside.

▌ Using a chopper, roughly mince prawn and mackerel together.

▌ Combine ground *rempah* paste, minced seafood and turmeric leaf in a mixing bowl. Season to taste with sugar and salt.

▌ Using a butter knife, spread a layer of seafood mixture in the middle of a coconut leaf. Carefully fold in half along the central stem.

▌ Double-wrap with another coconut leaf, with the stem of the second leaf facing the open side of filled coconut leaf.

▌ Secure both ends with bamboo skewers or cocktail sticks. Repeat until ingredients are used up.

▌ Pan-fry or charcoal-grill *otak-otak* for 5–8 minutes or until cooked, basting with oil and turning frequently to prevent burning.

▌ Serve warm.

Note: Otak-otak is a traditional Malay snack. Rempah is the Malay term for "spice paste".

Fried Spring Rolls Filled with Fish Paste and Salted Duck's Eggs

Spring roll wrappers	2, round and 23 cm (9-in) in diameter
Salted duck's egg yolks	6, left whole
Plain (all-purpose) flour	2 tsp, mixed with sufficient water to make a thick paste

Filling

Fish paste	350 g (12 oz)
Chinese chives (*ku cai*)	10 g (¹/₃ oz), chopped, about 4 Tbsp
Water chestnuts	5, peeled and chopped
Tapioca (cassava) flour	2 Tbsp
Sesame oil	1 tsp
Salt	1 tsp or to taste
Ground white pepper	¹/₄ tsp or to taste

▌ Combine all filling ingredients in a bowl. Mix well and season to taste. Set aside.

▌ To assemble, place a spring roll wrapper on a clean work surface and spread some filling along the centre.

▌ Top with 3 salted duck's egg yolks, then fold in left and right sides and roll up. Seal with flour paste. Repeat with remaining ingredients.

▌ Deep-fry each spring roll in moderately hot oil until light brown.

▌ Remove and drain on paper towels.

▌ Cut into desired serving-size pieces and serve warm.

Golden Seafood Balls

Prawn (shrimp) meat	300 g (10 oz), minced
Crab sticks	5, thinly sliced
Sesame oil	1 tsp
Water chestnuts	3, peeled and chopped
Egg white	1
Corn flour (cornstarch)	1 Tbsp
Chicken stock granules	1 tsp
Ground white pepper	1 tsp
Sugar	1 tsp or to taste
Salt	$^1/_2$ tsp or to taste
Frozen spring roll wrappers	1 packet, about 100 g (3$^1/_2$ oz), each 11.5 x 12.5 cm (4$^1/_2$ x 5 in), thawed and cut into 0.5-cm ($^1/_4$-in) strips
Cooking oil for deep-frying	

METHOD

▌ In a mixing bowl, combine prawns, crab sticks, sesame oil, water chestnuts, egg white, corn flour, chicken stock granules and pepper. Season to taste with sugar and salt.

▌ Place in the refrigerator to chill.

▌ Take about 1 Tbsp chilled seafood paste and shape into a ball roughly 3.5 cm (1$^1/_2$-in) in diameter. Repeat until paste is used up.

▌ Roll seafood balls in spring roll strips to coat.

▌ Heat cooking oil until moderately hot, then deep-fry seafood balls until golden brown.

▌ Drain on absorbent paper towels and serve immediately.

▌ If preferred, serve with dipping sauce for Fried Vietnamese Spring Rolls (pg 32) or dipping sauce of choice.

Tuna Spiral Puffs

INGREDIENTS

Canned tuna in mayonnaise	1 can, 175 g (6 oz), drained well
Onion	1, large, peeled and cubed
Sweet potato	200 g (7 oz), peeled, cubed and steamed until soft
Chopped spring onions (scallions)	2 Tbsp
Crab sticks	40 g (1¼ oz), sliced
Ground white pepper	¼ tsp
Cooking oil for deep-frying	

Water dough

Plain (all-purpose) flour	200 g (7 oz), sifted
Margarine	60 g (2 oz)
Cooking oil	1 Tbsp
Sugar	1 Tbsp
Water	45–50 ml (1⅓–2 fl oz)
Egg	½

Oil dough

Plain (all-purpose) flour	180 g (6 oz), sifted
Vegetable shortening	90 g (3 oz)
Salt	½ tsp

METHOD

▌ Prepare filling by mixing all ingredients, except oil for deep-frying, together. Set aside.

▌ Prepare water dough. Combine all ingredients and mix to form a soft dough, kneading until smooth. Cover dough with a tea towel and leave to rest for 30 minutes.

▌ Prepare oil dough. Combine all ingredients and mix to form a soft dough, then divide into 7 equal balls. Set aside.

▌ Divide water dough into 7 equal balls. Use a rolling pin to flatten each ball into a round large enough to wrap oil dough.

▌ Place a portion of oil dough onto the centre of each round of water dough, then gather up edges of water dough to wrap and seal.

▌ Flatten the filled dough into a rectangle about 7 x 3 cm (3 x 1½ in) using a rolling pin, then roll up Swiss-roll style starting from the shorter side.

▌ Flatten roll into a rectangle again, about 7 x 3 cm (3 x 1½ in), and roll up from the short side once more. Halve into 2 equal rounds.

▌ Place each portion of pastry, cut side up, on a work surface and use a rolling pin to flatten each into a larger round, about 7 cm (3 in) in diameter and 0.5-cm (¼-in) thick.

▌ Spoon 1 Tbsp filling onto the centre of a pastry round, then cover with other pastry round.

▌ Secure pastry 'sandwich' by pressing edges together and pinching in pleats to seal. Repeat until ingredients are used up.

▌ Deep-fry prepared puffs in a wok over medium heat until golden brown.

▌ Drain on paper towels and serve as a tea-time snack.

Fish Poached with Grapes

White fish fillets or steaks	2, each 150–180 g (5–6 oz), washed and patted dry with paper towels, use cod (*ikan cod*) or threadfin (*ikan kurau*)
Aluminium foil for wrapping	
Cooking oil for greasing	
Seedless green grapes	5
Seedless red grapes	5

Seasoning

Olive oil	1 Tbsp
Salt	1 tsp or to taste
Ground black pepper	½ tsp
Chinese cooking wine	1–2 Tbsp, or any table white wine

METHOD

▌ Combine seasoning ingredients, then add fish and coat well. Refrigerate for 30 minutes.

▌ Lightly grease foil with oil, then place grapes and fish, including combined seasoning ingredients, on top. Wrap up securely.

▌ Bake foil parcel in a preheated oven at 190°C (370°F) for 10 minutes or until fish is cooked.

▌ Remove fish, grapes and juices from foil and serve immediately.

Steamed Prawns with Jasmine Tea in Lotus Leaves

Prawns (shrimps)	350 g (12 oz), medium-size
Aluminium foil	
Lotus leaves	2, washed and soaked

Marinade

Jasmine tea leaves	10 g ($^1/_3$ oz), steeped in 60 ml (2 fl oz / 4 Tbsp) hot water
Abalone sauce	2 tsp
Sesame oil	1 tsp
Chinese cooking wine	1 Tbsp
Corn flour (cornstarch)	1 tsp
Ground white pepper	$^1/_4$ tsp
Light soy sauce	1 tsp
Salt	$^1/_2$ tsp or to taste

METHOD

❚ Devein and trim prawns if desired, but leave whole. Wash and drain, then set aside.

❚ Prepare marinade. Remove tea leaves from tea and discard. Mix tea with remaining marinade ingredients and season to taste.

❚ Place foil over a bowl large enough for prawns, then place cleaned lotus leaves on top. Add prawns and marinade.

❚ Fold in left and right edges of lotus leaves, then fold down upper edge and fold up lower edge; a rectangular parcel should result.

❚ Wrap foil over lotus leaves for added support and tie with kitchen string or twine to secure.

❚ Steam parcel over high heat for 10–12 minutes or until prawns are cooked. Be careful not to overcook prawns.

❚ Unwrap parcel and serve warm with steamed white rice.

Fried Shredded Cuttlefish and Vegetables

INGREDIENTS

Cooking oil	3 Tbsp
Garlic	2 cloves, peeled and chopped
Shallots	3, peeled and chopped
Preserved soy bean paste (*tau cheo*)	1 Tbsp
Chicken fillet	180 g (6 oz), julienned
Dried cuttlefish	150 g (5 oz), shredded, washed and mixed with 1 Tbsp vinegar
Dried shiitake mushrooms	6, soaked to soften, stems discarded and julienned
Yam bean (*bangkuang*)	450 g (1 lb), peeled
Carrot	1, peeled if desired and julienned
Cabbage	200 g (7 oz), finely shredded
Onions	2, large, peeled and sliced
Chicken stock	125–180 ml (4–6 fl oz)
Ground white pepper	1 tsp or to taste
Salt	1 tsp or to taste
Sugar	2 Tbsp or to taste
Spring onions (scallions)	10 g (1/3 oz), cut into 2.5-cm (1-in) lengths
Coriander leaves (cilantro)	10 g (1/3 oz), cut into 2.5-cm (1-in) lengths
Chinese lettuce	2–3 bunches, or 1 head of iceberg lettuce, whole leaves separated, washed and refrigerated

Sambal belacan (optional)

Fresh red chillies	8
Dried prawn (shrimp) paste (*belacan*)	2 Tbsp, toasted
Kalamansi lime (*limau kesturi*) juice	extracted from 3 limes

METHOD

▮ Heat oil in a wok over medium heat. Sauté garlic and shallots until fragrant.

▮ Add preserved soy bean paste and sauté for 30 seconds.

▮ Add chicken, cuttlefish, mushrooms, yam bean, carrot, cabbage and onions. Stir-fry until vegetables start to soften, adding just enough chicken stock to prevent vegetables from sticking to the wok. Leave to simmer for 8–10 minutes.

▮ Season to taste with pepper, salt and sugar. Stir in spring onions and coriander leaves, then remove from heat and set aside to cool.

▮ Prepare *sambal belacan*, if using. Pound chillies and dried prawn paste together until fine using a mortar and pestle. Mix in lime juice.

▮ Serve filling, lettuce leaves and *sambal belacan*, if using, separately. Allow diners to spoon desired amounts of filling, as well as *sambal belacan*, onto leaves, then wrap up to eat out of hand.

▮ For alternative presentation, stack 2 Chinese lettuce leaves, frilly ends away from each other, and spoon some filling along the centre. Fold frilly ends upwards and towards each other so a cup is formed, then tie with a scalded spring onion (scallion) to secure.

Note: The filling of this recipe was inspired by a traditional Peranakan or Straits Chinese dish called *joo hoo char*, which literally translates into "cuttlefish stir-fry" from Hokkien. To prepare chicken stock at home, chop up 1 cleaned chicken carcass and boil in 1 litre (32 fl oz / 4 cups) water over medium heat for 10–15 minutes, then strain before use. Alternatively, dissolve 2 tsp chicken stock granules in 125–180 ml (4–6 fl oz) water.

Fisherman's Catch

Cooking oil for greasing

Roti jala mould
  (see pg 142)

Fisherman's net

Plain (all-purpose) flour	250 g (9 oz)
Water	450 ml (15 fl oz / 1⁴/₅ cup)
Coconut milk	100 ml (3¹/₂ fl oz), squeezed from ¹/₂ grated coconut with sufficient water added
Eggs	3
Cooking oil	1 Tbsp
Salt	1 tsp

Filling

Cooking oil	2 Tbsp
Lemon grass (*serai*)	2 stalks, bruised
Onions	1, peeled and chopped
Black mustard seeds (*biji sawi*)	1 tsp
Fish curry powder	2 Tbsp, mixed with 200 ml (6¹/₂ fl oz) water
Torch ginger bud (*bunga kantan*)	1, thinly sliced
Pumpkin flesh	300 g (10 oz), cubed
Shelled prawns (shrimps)	200 g (7 oz), use medium-size prawns
Squid tubes	100 g (3¹/₂ oz), sliced into rings
Sugar	1 tsp or to taste
Salt	1 tsp or to taste

- Prepare fisherman's net. Combine all ingredients in a mixing bowl and stir to blend. Strain and leave to rest for 20 minutes.
- Heat an iron griddle or non-stick pan over low to medium heat and lightly grease with oil.
- Fill *roti jala* mould with some batter and move it over the pan in circles to create a lacy pancake.
- When batter is set, turn pancake over and cook until the edges leave the pan, takes ¹/₂–1 minute.
- Repeat until batter is used up.
- Prepare seafood filling. Heat oil in a pan, then add lemon grass, onions and mustard seeds. Sauté until fragrant.
- Add curry powder paste, torch ginger bud and pumpkin. Cook until pumpkin is done, about 2 minutes. Add more water if necessary.
- Once mixture is reduced, add seafood and season to taste with sugar and salt.
- When seafood is cooked, remove from heat and leave to cool.
- To serve, place a lacy pancake on a clean plate and top with 2 Tbsp seafood mixture on one half of pancake.
- Fold pancake in half to cover the filling, then fold pancake semicircle in thirds to form a pointed tip at the centre.
- Serve immediately.
- An alternative serving suggestion is to place 1 Tbsp filling near one edge of lacy pancake. Fold lower edge over ingredients, then fold in left and right sides and roll up to resemble a spring roll.

Steamed Seafood Otak-otak

Fish fillet	300 g (10 oz), sliced, use threadfin (*ikan kurau*), grouper (*ikan kerapu*) or mangrove snapper (*ikan jenahak*)
Prawn (shrimp) meat	150 g (5 oz)
Squid tubes	150 g (5 oz), sliced into rings
Cooking oil	1 Tbsp
Salt	1/2 tsp
Sugar	1 tsp
Rice flour	1 1/2 Tbsp
Eggs	3
Banana leaves	4 large leaves, cut into 10 circles, each 22 cm (9 in) in diameter, and scalded to soften
Stapler and staples	
Basil leaves	1/2 cup (15–20 g)
Shredded kaffir lime leaves for garnishing	

Rempah

Lemon grass (*serai*)	2 stalks, sliced
Dried chillies	10, soaked
Shallots	5, peeled and sliced
Garlic	2 cloves, peeled and sliced
Turmeric (*kunyit*)	2.5-cm (1-in) knob, peeled
Galangal (*lengkuas*)	2.5-cm (1-in) knob, peeled
Kaffir lime leaves (*daun limau purut*)	5–6
Black peppercorns	5
Dried prawn (shrimp) paste (*belacan*)	1/2 tsp
Pure coconut cream (*pati santan*)	300 ml (10 fl oz), squeezed from 1 grated coconut
Palm sugar (*gula Melaka*)	1 Tbsp
Fish sauce	2 Tbsp

METHOD

- Season seafood with oil, salt and sugar. Refrigerate for 30 minutes.

- Combine *rempah* ingredients using a blender (processor) until a paste forms.

- Transfer *rempah* paste to a mixing bowl. Mix in rice flour and eggs, then season to taste. Stir in seasoned seafood.

- Stack 2 banana leaf circles, one on top of the other, then fold them into a bowl with a squarish base—imagine a square at the centre of banana leaf circle, then fold leaf along 2 sides of the square and staple the corner to secure. Repeat with remaining sides.

- Place a few basil leaves into each banana leaf bowl and fill with seafood mixture. Repeat until ingredients are used up.

- Steam *otak-otak* over rapidly boiling water for 10–12 minutes or until cooked.

- Garnish and serve with steamed white rice.

Vegetables

Lotus Leaves

Aubergine Rolls
with Herbed Cheese Filling

Aubergines (eggplants/brinjals)	2, medium-size, each about 200 g (7 oz)
Olive oil for brushing	
Salt	to taste

Fresh tomato sauce

Olive oil	3 Tbsp
Garlic	1 clove, peeled and chopped
Dried chilli flakes	$\frac{1}{4}$ tsp
Plum (Roma) tomatoes	200 g (7 oz), chopped
Salt	1 tsp or to taste
Sugar	1 tsp or to taste

Cheese filling

Philadelphia cream cheese	150 g (5 oz)
Yoghurt	2 Tbsp
Finely chopped dill or herb of choice	3 tsp + more for garnishing
Freshly ground black pepper	$\frac{1}{4}$ tsp

METHOD

▌ Prepare eggplant. Peel 4-cm (2-in) wide strips of skin from opposite sides of each aubergine and discard.

▌ Holding a knife parallel to a peeled side, cut each aubergine lengthways into 8–10 slices, each 0.75-cm ($\frac{3}{8}$-in) thick. Alternatively, use a Y-shaped vegetable peeler with some pressure for similar slices.

▌ Brush both sides of slices with olive oil and season to taste with salt.

▌ Grill slices over charcoal heat, turning over once, until golden brown and tender. Alternatively, place a piece of wire mesh over a gas hob and grill over flames.

▌ Prepare tomato sauce. Heat oil in a pan. Sauté garlic and chilli flakes until garlic is golden.

▌ Add tomatoes, salt and sugar. Simmer, uncovered and stirring occasionally, until sauce slightly thickens; this takes 5–10 minutes.

▌ Prepare filling. Combine all ingredients in a bowl and stir to mix well.

▌ To assemble, divide cheese mixture among grilled aubergine slices and roll up.

▌ Serve rolls with sauce and garnished with extra dill.

Stuffed Bamboo Pith

INGREDIENTS

Bamboo pith (*chuk sang*)	15 g ($^1/_2$ oz), soaked to soften
Cooking oil	3 Tbsp
Garlic	2 cloves, peeled and chopped
Vegetarian ham	80 g (3 oz), cut into 5-cm (2-in) strips
Chicken stock	250 ml (8 fl oz / 1 cup)
Oyster sauce	1 tsp
Sesame oil	1 tsp
Celery	100 g ($3^1/_2$ oz), cut into 5-cm (2-in) lengths
Carrot	50 g (2 oz), cut into 5-cm (2-in) lengths
Asparagus	10, cut into 5-cm (2-in) lengths
Corn flour (cornstarch)	1 tsp, mixed with 2 Tbsp water
Chinese chives (*ku cai*)	as required, blanched to soften for tying

METHOD

▌ Scald bamboo pith to make sure they are fully rehydrated and softened. Drain and cut into 2-cm (1-in) lengths when cooled.

▌ Heat oil in a pan and sauté garlic until light brown and crisp. Remove and set aside.

▌ Using oil left in the pan, fry ham until fragrant. Remove and set aside.

▌ Combine chicken stock, oyster sauce and sesame oil in a saucepan. Bring to the boil and blanch vegetables for 5 seconds. Drain and set aside.

▌ Add corn flour solution to the stock. Once stock thickens, remove from heat and set aside.

▌ Stuff each bamboo pith length with one length of each blanched vegetable and vegetarian ham. Tie with softened Chinese chives to secure.

▌ Arrange on a platter and steam for 5 minutes over rapidly boiling water.

▌ Remove from steamer, pour stock over and top with garlic crisps.

▌ Serve immediately with steamed white rice.

▌ Alternatively, serve gravy separately and on the side for diners to adjust to their tastes.

Note: For home-made chicken stock, see pg 60 for instructions.

Mango Wraps with Peanut Sauce

INGREDIENTS

Shallots	6, peeled
Garlic	3 cloves, peeled
Bird's eye chillies (*cili padi*)	3 + more for garnishing
Skinned peanuts (groundnuts)	4 Tbsp, roasted and coarsely ground
Water	200 ml (6^1/$_2$ fl oz)
Fish sauce	2 Tbsp
Palm sugar (*gula Melaka*)	80 g (3 oz)
Chinese lettuce	2 bunches, leaves separated, or bok choy
Mangoes	2, firm, not too ripe, peeled and finely sliced lengthways
Grated skinned coconut	100 g (3^1/$_2$ oz)
Thai sweet basil keaves	2 cups (about 80 g)
Limes (*limau nipis*) (optional)	8, halved

METHOD

▌ Combine shallots, garlic and 3 chillies in a blender (processor) until they are well chopped, but not puréed.

▌ Combine peanuts, blended mixture, water, fish sauce and palm sugar in a saucepan. Bring to the boil and simmer for 10–15 minutes or until thick, dark and glossy.

▌ Transfer cooked mixture to a small serving bowl and set aside.

▌ Place a slice of mango on a clean work surface, lay a leaf of lettuce or bok choy on top and spoon some peanut sauce along the centre.

▌ Top with some coconut, basil and a squeeze of lime, if using. Add, if desired, a few slices of bird's eye chillies for both colour and added fieriness.

▌ Roll up and enjoy.

Note: **This is a dish redolent of piquant Thai flavours. It can be served as an appetiser or side dish.**

Yam Balls

INGREDIENTS

Peeled yam (taro)	150 g (5 oz), finely shredded
Chinese five-spice powder	$\frac{1}{8}$ tsp (a pinch)
White sesame seeds	1 tsp
Salt	$\frac{1}{4}$ tsp or to taste
Cooking oil for deep-frying	

Chicken balls

Chicken thigh meat	250 g (9 oz), minced
Corn flour (cornstarch)	2 tsp
Ground white pepper	1 tsp
Egg	1
Garlic	1, peeled and finely chopped
Celery	1 Tbsp, finely sliced
Chicken stock granules	1 tsp
Salt	1 tsp or to taste

Dipping sauce

Shallots	2, peeled and sliced
Garlic	1 clove, peeled and chopped
Bird's eye chillies (cili padi)	3, sliced
Lime (limau nipis) juice	75 ml (2$\frac{1}{2}$ fl oz / 5 Tbsp)
Brown sugar	1 tsp or to taste
Fish sauce	1 tsp

METHOD

▮ Combine all chicken ball ingredients in a mixing bowl. Season to taste and refrigerate, covered with cling film (plastic wrap), until needed.

▮ Combine all dipping sauce ingredients in a bowl and season to taste. Set aside.

▮ Mix shredded yam with five-spice powder, sesame seeds and salt.

▮ Portion chicken mixture into balls the size of kalamansi limes (limau kesturi) and roll in shredded yam.

▮ Deep-fry coated balls over low heat until golden brown. Drain on absorbent paper towels.

▮ Serve with dipping sauce.

Popiah

Plain (all-purpose) flour	320 g (10¹/₂ oz)
Salt	¹/₂ tsp
Water	250 ml (8 fl oz / 1 cup)

Filling

Yam beans (*bangkuang*)	1 kg (2 lb 3 oz)
Carrots	100 g (3¹/₂ oz)
Long (snake) beans	4
Cooking oil	3 Tbsp
Garlic	2 cloves, peeled and chopped
Shallots	2, peeled and chopped
Preserved soy bean paste (*tau cheo*)	1 Tbsp
Chicken thigh meat	200 g (7 oz), minced
Chicken stock granules	1 tsp
Salt	2 tsp or to taste
Sugar	60 ml (2 fl oz / 4 Tbsp) or to taste
Ground white pepper	1 tsp or to taste

Garnishing

Sweetened soy sauce (*tee cheo*)	100 g (3¹/₂ oz)
Garlic	8 cloves, peeled and pounded until fine
Red chillies	8, pounded until fine with ¹/₂ tsp salt
Chinese lettuce	1–2 bunches, leaves separated, washed and drained
Crabmeat	200 g (7 oz), cooked
Prawn (shrimps) meat	200 g (7 oz), cooked
Firm bean curd (*tau kwa*)	1 piece, chopped and pan-fried with a little oil
Bean sprouts	100 g (3¹/₂ oz), scalded
Cucumber	1, peeled if desired and julienned
Chinese celery	1 sprig or to taste, finely sliced
Shallots	10, peeled, sliced and crisp-fried

METHOD

- Prepare *popiah* skins. Mix plain flour, salt and water together in a bowl, then leave to rest for 3 hours.

- Beat batter using an electric mixer fitted with a dough hook attachment, then cover with a tea towel and set aside for 1 hour.

- Heat a non-stick pan over low heat. Hold dough in your palm and in a circular motion, quickly smear a thin round of batter onto the pan.

- Cook until skin starts to leave the sides of pan, then quickly remove and transfer to a plate. Cover with a tea towel. Repeat until dough is used up.

- Prepare filling ingredients. Peel and julienne yam beans, then wash and drain in a colander until dry. Peel carrots, if desired, then julienne and set aside. Slice cleaned long beans and set aside.

- Prepare filling. Heat oil in a wok and stir-fry garlic and shallots until fragrant.

- Add soy bean paste and stir-fry until fragrant again. Stir in chicken, chicken stock granules, yam beans, carrots and long beans.

- Season to taste with salt, sugar and pepper. Cook until vegetables are done, about 10 minutes, then remove from heat

- To assemble, place a *popiah* skin on a plate. Spread on some sweetened soy sauce and pounded garlic and chillies.

- Place a lettuce leaf on top and add on 1–2 Tbsp filling. Top with a little of each remaining garnishing ingredient.

- Fold in left and right sides of skin, then roll up into a cylindrical shape.

- Serve *popiah* roll whole or cut into 4–5 pieces.

Note: Popiah is Hokkien for "thin pancake", which is used to wrap a rich combination of ingredients in this traditional dish. Making popiah skins requires some skill and considerable effort. To save time, buy ready-made ones from wet markets or frozen ones from supermarkets, if preferred.

Grilled Bean Curd Puffs

Bean curd puffs (*tau pok*) 10, large, each about 7 x 7 cm (3 x 3 in)

Red chillies 6, seeded, sliced and pounded until fine

Skinned peanuts
(groundnuts) 100 g (3¹/₂ oz), roasted and coarsely crushed

Sauce

Palm sugar (*gula Melaka*) 150 g (5 oz), chopped

Castor (superfine) sugar 2 Tbsp

Dark soy sauce 3 Tbsp

Dried prawn (shrimp)
paste (*belacan*) 1 tsp, toasted

Tamarind pulp
(*asam Jawa*) 1 Tbsp, mixed with 60 ml (2 fl oz / 4 Tbsp) water and strained for juice

Filling

Cucumber 1, peeled if desired and julienned

Bean sprouts 100 g (3¹/₂ oz), tailed if desired and scalded

Yam bean (*bangkuang*) 50 g (2 oz), peeled and julienned

METHOD

▌ Prepare sauce. Combine both sugars in a saucepan and cook over low heat until dissolved. Strain syrup into a clean saucepan.

▌ Add all remaining ingredients and simmer for 5 minutes or until sauce thickens. Remove from heat and set aside.

▌ Slit bean curd puffs horizontally on one side to make a pocket. Stuff with filling ingredients.

▌ Lightly grill filled bean curd puffs over charcoal heat until light brown, turning over once. Alternatively, pan-fry on an oiled griddle.

▌ Either leave whole or slice into quarters and place on a serving plate.

▌ Pour sauce over and top with desired amounts of pounded chillies and peanuts. Serve warm.

Thai Pepper Leaf Wraps

INGREDIENTS

Pointed pepper leaves
(*daun kaduk*) .... as required

Sauce

Palm sugar (*gula Melaka*) .... 200 g (7 oz), chopped

Water .... 125 ml (4 fl oz / ½ cup)

Fish sauce .... 2 Tbsp

Dried prawn shrimp
paste (*belacan*) .... 1 tsp

Shallots .... 3, left whole and unpeeled

Ginger .... 1.5-cm (¾-in) knob, left
                               whole and unpeeled

Galangal (*lengkuas*) .... 2-cm (1-in) knob, left whole
                               and unpeeled

Grated skinned coconut .... 50 g (2 oz)

Skinned peanuts
(groundnuts) .... 50 g (2 oz)

Filling

Shallots .... 8, peeled and sliced

Limes (*limau nipis*) .... 4–5, cored, seeded and cubed
                               with skin intact

Bird's eye chillies
(*cili padi*) .... 10, sliced

Dried prawns (shrimps) .... 3 Tbsp, washed and roasted in
                               a dry pan

Lemon grass (*serai*) .... 4 stalks, thinly sliced

Skinned peanuts
(groundnuts) .... 150 g (5 oz), roasted and used
                               whole

Grated skinned coconut .... 100 g (3½ oz), roasted in a
                               dry wok until lightly browned

Young ginger .... 10 g (⅓ oz), peeled and cubed

METHOD

▌ Prepare sauce. Combine palm sugar and water in a saucepan. Boil until sugar dissolves and syrup thickens. Remove from heat and stir in fish sauce.

▌ Individually roast dried prawn paste, shallots, ginger and galangal until slightly charred, either over charcoal heat or over a gas hob with a wire mesh on top. Alternatively, hold each ingredient with tongs and roast directly over an open flame.

▌ Peel cooled, roasted shallots, ginger and galangal. Set aside.

▌ Separately toast grated coconut and peanuts in a dry wok until light brown.

▌ Combine dried prawn paste, shallots, ginger, galangal, grated coconut and peanuts in a blender (processor) until fine.

▌ Transfer blended mixture to a serving bowl and mix in palm sugar syrup. Set aside.

▌ Arrange pepper leaves, filling ingredients and prepared sauce on a large serving platter.

▌ To serve, put a little of each filling ingredient onto a pepper leaf. Drizzle on some sauce, then wrap up and eat.

Note: The Thai people know this dish as *mieng kam.*

Vegetarian Samosas

Popiah **skins** — 10

Filling

Cooking oil	2 Tbsp
Brown mustard seeds (*biji sawi*)	1 tsp
Fennel seeds (*jintan manis biji*)	1/4 tsp
Garlic	1 clove, peeled and chopped
Onion	1, large, peeled and diced
Fish curry powder	3 Tbsp, mixed with 4 Tbsp water to make a paste
Pumpkin	350 g (12 oz), peeled and diced
Water	80–100 ml (2 1/2–3 1/2 fl oz)
Green peas	50 g (2 oz)
Coconut cream	2 Tbsp
Curry leaves	2 sprigs
Salt	1 tsp or to taste

METHOD

▌ Prepare filling. Heat oil in a pan and add mustard and fennel seeds. Cook until oil sizzles.

▌ Add garlic and onion and sauté until onion is soft.

▌ Add curry paste and sauté until fragrant. Stir in pumpkin and water.

▌ Cook until pumpkin is soft; this takes 5–8 minutes.

▌ Mix in green peas, coconut cream, curry leaves and season to taste.

▌ Once mixture becomes thick and gravy is mostly absorbed, turn off heat and set aside to cool.

▌ Wrap samosas as shown on pg 144.

▌ Deep-fry triangular parcels until light golden. Remove and drain on absorbent paper towels.

Rice and Noodles

Bamboo Leaves

Turmeric Rice and Chicken Curry Dumplings

INGREDIENTS

Glutinous rice	1 kg (2 lb 3 oz), washed and drained
Ground turmeric (*kunyit serbuk*)	2 rounded (heaped) Tbsp
Dried sour fruit (*asam gelugur*)	2–3 pieces
Coconut milk	250 ml (8 fl oz / 1 cup)
White peppercorns	1 tsp
Salt	1 rounded (heaped) tsp
Bamboo leaves	30–40, washed and soaked to soften
Dried Chinese chestnuts	150 g (5 oz), soaked, parboiled and cleaned
Hemp strings for tying	

Filling

Cooking oil	125 ml (4 fl oz / ½ cup)
Star anise	3
Cinnamon stick	1, 5-cm (2-in) length
Cardamoms	3
Onions	4, large, peeled and sliced
Garlic	3 cloves, peeled and chopped
Red chillies	2, coarsely chopped
Meat curry powder	120 g (4 oz), mixed with 500 ml (16 fl oz / 2 cups) water
Chicken breast meat	1 kg (2 lb 3 oz), cut into bite-size cubes
Chicken stock granules	2 tsp
Coconut milk	125 ml, squeezed from ½ grated coconut with sufficient water added
Curry leaves	2 sprigs
Sugar	2 Tbsp or to taste
Salt	1 Tbsp or to taste

METHOD

▌ Prepare glutinous rice. Soak washed rice in water mixed with ground turmeric and dried sour fruit slices overnight.

▌ Wash soaked rice in several changes of water, then drain.

▌ Combine coconut milk, peppercorns, salt and washed rice in a mixing bowl. Set aside for 1 hour for the flavours to infuse.

▌ Meanwhile, prepare filling. Heat oil in a wok and fry spices briefly. Add onions, garlic and chillies and sauté until fragrant.

▌ Add curry powder paste and sauté until fragrant, then add chicken, chicken stock granules, coconut milk and curry leaves. Bring to the boil, stirring continuously.

▌ Reduce heat and cook until chicken is done. Add sugar and salt to taste, then remove from heat and set aside.

▌ To assemble, overlap 2 bamboo leaves lengthways and fold into a cone as shown on pg 145.

▌ Fill cone with 1 rounded (heaped) tsp turmeric rice. Add 2 rounded Tbsp filling and 2–3 chestnuts, followed by another 2 heaped Tbsp turmeric rice.

▌ Fold bamboo leaves over to cover rice, then fold to form a pyramid shape and tie tightly with hemp string to secure.

▌ Repeat until ingredients are used up; this recipe makes 15–20 dumplings.

▌ Lower dumplings into a large pot of boiling water and cook for 2–2¼ hours or until done.

▌ Drain dumplings and hang them up to dry. Serve.

Note: Turmeric rice, or *nasi kunyit*, and chicken curry are two dishes that were customarily served side by side. Here, the two have been combined into a singular item.

Nasi Lemak Bungkus

INGREDIENTS

Long grain rice	400 g (13½ oz)
Coconut milk	250 ml (8 fl oz / 1 cup), squeezed from 1 grated coconut with sufficient water added
Water	400 ml (13 fl oz)
Salt	1 tsp or to taste
Screwpine (*pandan*) leaves	2, knotted
Banana leaves	10, each 22 x 22 cm (9 x 9 in)

Condiments

Sambal (see recipe below)

Deep-fried anchovies

Sliced cucumber

Sliced hard-boiled eggs

Sambal

Red chillies	5
Dried chillies	50 g (2 oz), pre-soaked and cut into 2.5-cm (1-in) lengths
Shallots	5, peeled and sliced
Garlic	1 clove, peeled and sliced
Dried prawn (shrimp) paste (*belacan*)	1 tsp, toasted
Cooking oil	125 ml (4 fl oz / ½ cup)
Onion	1, large, peeled and sliced
Sugar	to taste
Salt	to taste

METHOD

▌ Wash rice in several changes of water until water runs clear. Drain.

▌ In an electric rice cooker, combine rice, coconut milk, water, salt and screwpine leaves. Mix well, then set appliance to cook rice.

▌ When done, use a fork to fluff up rice. Leave rice to rest for 10–15 minutes, covered in the electric cooker, before use.

▌ To assemble, scoop 1 bowl or 1 cup of rice onto the centre of a banana leaf, then add desired amounts of condiments.

▌ Fold as shown for *pulut inti* on pg 146, only enclose rice completely.

▌ To prepare *sambal*, combine both chillies, shallots, garlic, dried prawn paste and half the oil in a blender (processor) until a fine paste forms.

▌ Heat remaining oil in a wok and cook blended paste over low heat until fragrant and oil separates.

▌ Add sliced onion and season to taste with salt and sugar. Cook until onion slices are soft.

▌ Turn off heat, dish out and serve with *nasi lemak* above.

Note: Nasi lemak bungkus, or wrapped coconut rice, is a classic Malay dish and can be thought of as early take-out food. *Nasi lemak* is typically eaten for breakfast. For a more traditional look, cut a few sheets of newspaper into 23 x 18 cm (9 x 7 in) pieces, and place a sheet under each banana leaf to fold together. The addition of a newpaper layer helps to prevent leakages should the banana leaf tear in parts.

Savoury Beef Rendang Pillows

INGREDIENTS

Glutinous rice	1 kg (2 lb 3 oz), soaked in water overnight and drained
Black-eyed beans	5 Tbsp, soaked in water for 3 hours and drained
Coconut cream	75 ml (2½ fl oz / 5 Tbsp)
Salt	1 rounded (heaped) tsp or to taste
Bamboo leaves	16–20, washed and soaked
Hemp strings	8–10, washed and soaked

Rempah

Dried red chillies	30, pre-soaked
Onions	5, large, peeled
Fresh ginger	5-cm (2-in) knob, peeled
Lemon grass (*serai*)	6 stalks, sliced
Turmeric (*kunyit*)	2.5-cm (1-in) knob, peeled
Water	250 ml (8 fl oz / 1 cup)

Filling

Stewing beef	1 kg (2 lb 3 oz), cut into bite-size cubes
Coconut milk	1 litre (32 fl oz / 4 cups), squeezed from 2 grated coconuts with sufficient water added
Freshly grated coconut	100 g (3½ oz), toasted brown in a dry pan, then blended (processed) until fine
Tamarind pulp (*asam Jawa*)	2 Tbsp, mixed with 125 ml (4 fl oz / ½ cup) water and strained for juice
Turmeric leaves (*daun kunyit*)	2, thinly sliced
Kaffir lime leaves (*daun limau purut*)	4–6
Sugar	2 Tbsp or to taste
Salt	2 Tbsp or to taste

METHOD

▌ Prepare *rempah*. Combine all *rempah* ingredients in a blender (processor) or pound with a mortar and pestle until a fine paste forms.

▌ Prepare filling. With *rempah* paste in a wok, add beef and coconut milk. Bring to the boil, stirring continuously, then reduce heat to medium.

▌ Continue to cook until beef is tender and liquid almost completely absorbed.

▌ Add toasted coconut, tamarind juice, turmeric and kaffir lime leaves, then season to taste with salt and sugar. Cook for 5 minutes, then turn off heat. Set aside.

▌ Prepare rice. Drain the glutinous rice and black-eyed beans in a colander.

▌ Combine rice, black-eyed beans, coconut cream and salt in a mixing bowl. Set aside.

▌ To assemble, take 2 large bamboo leaves and overlap them lengthways.

▌ Spoon 2 rounded (heaped) Tbsp glutinous rice mixture onto the centre of the bamboo leaves, then top with 3 rounded tsp filling.

▌ Cover filling with 2 rounded Tbsp glutinous rice mixture.

▌ Fold leaves into a rectangular dumpling, then tie with hemp string to secure as shown on pg 145. Repeat until ingredients are used up.

▌ Lower dumplings into a large pot of boiling water and cook for 1¾–2 hours or until cooked.

▌ Drain dumplings and hang up to drain off excess water. Serve.

Note: Pillow dumplings are elongated glutinous rice dumplings of Chinese origin, while beef *rendang* is a traditional Malay dish of spicy, stewed beef cubes.

Thai Basil Fried Rice

INGREDIENTS

Chicken meat	150 g (5 oz), preferably thigh meat, diced
Cooking oil	3 Tbsp
Garlic	1 clove, peeled and chopped
Button mushrooms	5, diced
Long (snake) beans	50 g (2 oz), sliced
Bird's eye chillies (*cili padi*)	3, or to taste, sliced
Fish sauce	3 Tbsp
Palm sugar (*gula Melaka*)	1 Tbsp
Ground white pepper	$\frac{1}{2}$ tsp
Salt	1 tsp or to taste
Cooked rice	300 g (10 oz)
Thai sweet basil leaves	$\frac{1}{2}$ cup (about 20 g) or to taste
Crisp-fried shallots	2 Tbsp
Chinese cabbage leaves	6, scalded to soften in 1 litre (32 fl oz / 4 cups) water with 1 Tbsp sugar added
Thai sweet basil leaves for garnishing	

Seasoning

Corn flour (cornstarch)	1 tsp
Sesame oil	1 tsp
Salt	$\frac{1}{8}$ tsp (a pinch)
Ground black pepper	$\frac{1}{8}$ tsp (a pinch)

METHOD

▌ Mix chicken with seasoning ingredients and refrigerate for 20 minutes.

▌ In a wok, heat oil and sauté garlic until fragrant.

▌ Stir in seasoned chicken and sauté for 30 seconds or until chicken is cooked.

▌ Add mushrooms, long beans, chillies, fish sauce and palm sugar. Season to taste with white pepper and salt. Continue stir-frying over high heat for 1 minute.

▌ Add cooked rice and stir-fry until fragrant.

▌ Turn off heat, then stir in basil leaves and crisp-fried shallots.

▌ To assemble, place 3 softened cabbage leaves into a bowl as shown on pg 145.

▌ Add 1 bowl or 1 cup of fried rice at the centre, then fold in one leaf to cover rice and the other two leaves over it. Repeat with second bowl.

▌ Place prepared bowls onto a steaming tray and steam over high heat for 5 minutes.

▌ To serve, cover each bowl with a serving dish and turn over. Garnish and serve immediately.

▌ Alternatively, spoon rice into individual serving bowls and garnish as desired. The mild sweetness from the cabbage leaves would have infused the rice.

Nyonya Dumplings

Glutinous rice	500 g (1 lb 1½ oz), washed and soaked in water overnight
Glutinous rice	50 g (2 oz), washed and soaked in water with a little blue food colouring overnight
Dried bamboo leaves	24–30, washed and soaked
Screwpine (*pandan*) leaf	3–4, washed and cut into 5-cm (2-in) lengths
Hemp strings for tying	2 bunches

Filling

Cooking oil	100 ml (3½ oz)
Garlic	2, peeled and chopped
Shallots	4, peeled and chopped
Preserved soy bean paste (*tau cheo*)	2 tsp
Ground coriander (*ketumbar serbuk*)	5–6 rounded (heaped) Tbsp, mixed with 125 ml (4 fl oz / ½ cup) water
Chicken breast meat	500 g (1 lb 1½ oz), cut into 1.5-cm (¾-in) cubes
Dried Chinese mushrooms	10, soaked to soften and cubed
Candied winter melon (*tung kwa tong*)	80 g (3 oz), cubed
Dark soy sauce	1 Tbsp
Ground white pepper	2 tsp
Sugar	60 ml (2 fl oz / 4 Tbsp) or to taste
Salt	2 tsp or to taste

METHOD

▌ Prepare filling. Heat oil in wok and stir-fry garlic and shallots until fragrant.

▌ Add soy bean and coriander pastes. Continue sautéing until fragrant.

▌ Add chicken, mushrooms and winter melon. Season with soy sauce and pepper, as well as sugar and salt to taste.

▌ Turn off heat once chicken is cooked. Set aside to cool.

▌ To assemble, overlap 2 bamboo leaves lengthways and fold into a cone as shown on pg 145.

▌ Fill base of cone with a little blue glutinous rice, if using, or just plain glutinous rice.

▌ Spoon 2 rounded (heaped) Tbsp filling over rice and cover with more glutinous rice. Top with a length of screwpine leaf.

▌ Fold down bamboo leaves to cover rice, then fold to form a pyramid shape and tie tightly with hemp string to secure.

▌ Repeat until ingredients are used up; this recipe makes 12–15 dumplings.

▌ Bring a large pot of salted water to the boil. Completely immerse dumplings in rapidly boiling water and cook for 2–2¼ hours.

▌ Once cooked, drain dumplings and hang up to drip off excess water before eating or storing.

Note: Although the pyramid-shaped dumpling is Chinese in origin, Peranakan or Straits Chinese cooks in Southeast Asia have since given it their own twist, hence Nyonya dumplings. Apart from store-bought blue food colouring, a natural alternative can be made by simmering 50 g (2 oz) of dried clitoria petals (*bunga terlang*) in 100 ml (3½ fl oz) of water. Simmer for about 3 minutes, turn off heat and squeeze petals to extract as much colour as possible, then use immediately.

Vietnamese Rice Paper Rolls

INGREDIENTS

Chicken fillet or beef	100 g (3½ oz)
Salt	2 tsp or to taste
Prawn (shrimp) meat	200 g (7 oz)
Vietnamese rice paper	12 sheets
Chinese lettuce	12 leaves, or salad leaves of choice
Transparent (glass) noodles (*tang hoon*)	100 g (3½ oz), blanched in hot water to soften and drained well
Bean sprouts	100 g (3½ oz), tailed if desired, scalded briefly in hot water and drained
Fresh basil leaves	½ cup (about 20 g)
Mint leaves	½ cup (about 20 g)
Carrot	50 g (2 oz), peeled if desired and shredded
Fresh coriander leaves (cilantro)	2 sprigs, shredded
Water	

Dipping Sauce

Kalamansi lime (*limau kesturi*) juice	extracted from 2–3 limes
Water	2 Tbsp
Sugar	80–100 g (2–3½ oz) or to taste
Fish sauce	2 Tbsp
Garlic	1 clove, peeled and chopped
Bird's eye chillies (*cili padi*)	2–3, chopped

METHOD

▌ Prepare dipping sauce. Combine lime juice, water and sugar in a bowl and stir until sugar dissolves. Adjust to taste with fish sauce and set aside.

▌ Bring a saucepan of water to a boil. Add meat and salt. Boil until meat is fully cooked.

▌ Remove meat from water and leave to cool. Slice cooled meat into strips and set aside.

▌ Return the same pot of water to the boil. Add prawns and simmer until cooked. Remove and arrange beside chicken slices.

▌ To assemble, moisten rice paper with some water and lay over a clean kitchen towel.

▌ Place a lettuce or salad leaf on the bottom third of the paper.

▌ Top with 2 pieces of chicken, 2 prawns, some transparent noodles, bean sprouts, basil and mint leaves, carrot and coriander.

▌ Fold bottom edge of rice paper over filling, then fold in left and right sides and roll up. Repeat until ingredients are used up.

▌ Place rolls on a serving plate, then finish dipping sauce by mixing in garlic and chillies. Serve.

Glutinous Rice in Lotus Leaves

INGREDIENTS

Cooking oil	2 Tbsp
Garlic	2 cloves, peeled and chopped
Shallots	2, peeled and chopped
Glutinous rice	600 g (1 lb 5 oz), washed, soaked in water overnight and drained before use
Lotus leaves	6, washed and soaked to soften
Salted duck's egg yolks	3
Dried chestnuts	12, soaked and cleaned
Black shiitake mushrooms	10, soaked to soften, stems discarded and quartered
Black-eyed beans	100 g (3$^1/_2$ oz), cooked in lightly salted water until soft
Hemp strings for tying	

Filling

Cooking oil	3 Tbsp
Garlic	2 cloves, peeled and chopped
Shallots	5, peeled and chopped
Dried prawns (shrimps) (*hae be*)	100 g (3$^1/_2$ oz), washed and drained
Chinese five-spice powder	1$^1/_2$ tsp
Chicken meat	500 g (1 lb 1$^1/_2$ oz), preferably thigh meat, cut into bite-size pieces
Dark soy sauce	1 tsp
Oyster sauce	1 Tbsp
Ground white pepper	$^1/_4$ tsp

Seasoning

Oyster sauce	1 tsp
Dark soy sauce	1 tsp
Chicken stock granules	1 tsp
Ground white pepper	a dash
Salt	to taste

METHOD

▌ Prepare filling. In a wok, heat 1 Tbsp oil and sauté a bit of garlic and shallots, as well as dried prawns until fragrant and prawns start to pop in the wok.

▌ Season with a dash of Chinese five-spice powder. Dish out and set aside.

▌ Heat remaining oil and sauté remaining garlic and shallots until fragrant.

▌ Stir in chicken, dark soy sauce, oyster sauce, remaining five-spice powder and pepper.

▌ Cook for 1 minute, then dish out and divide into 3 equal portions. Set aside.

▌ In a clean wok, heat 2 Tbsp oil and sauté garlic and shallots until fragrant.

▌ Add glutinous rice and seasoning ingredients. Cook for 1 minute, then dish out and divide rice into 3 equal portions.

▌ Line a large bowl with 2 lotus leaves. From one portion of the rice, scoop out 2–3 Tbsp and place onto lotus leaves.

▌ Top with one portion of chicken filling, 1 salted egg yolk and 4 chestnuts, as well as one-third of mushrooms and black-eyed beans.

▌ Cover with remaining glutinous rice from the single portion.

▌ Wrap rice up in lotus leaves to form a squarish parcel and tie with hemp strings to secure.

▌ Repeat with remaining ingredients to make 2 more parcels.

▌ Bring a large stockpot of water to a boil with 1 Tbsp salt.

▌ Lower in glutinous rice parcels and cook for 3 hours or until done, topping up with more hot water when necessary.

▌ When done, drain parcels and leave to cool. Serve warm or at room temperature.

Sweets

Banana Leaves

Green Tea Dumplings in Syrup

INGREDIENTS

Green tea powder	1 tsp
Green tea paste	1 Tbsp
Water	200 ml (6¹/₂ fl oz)
Glutinous rice flour	200 g (7 oz), sifted
Toasted sesame seeds for garnishing	

Syrup

Palm sugar (*gula Melaka*)	200 g (7 oz)
Rock sugar	50 g (2 oz)
Water	750 ml (24 fl oz / 3 cups)
Ginger	50 g (2 oz), peeled and sliced
Screwpine (*pandan*) leaves	2, washed and knotted

Filling

Cooking oil for deep-frying	
Skinned peanuts (groundnuts)	100 g (3¹/₂ oz)
Castor (superfine) sugar	50 g (2 oz)

METHOD

▌ Prepare syrup. Combine both sugars and water in a small pot. Simmer until sugars are dissolved. Strain into a clean pot.

▌ Add ginger and screwpine leaves. Simmer for 10 minutes over low heat. Remove and set aside.

▌ Prepare green tea dumplings. Combine green tea powder and paste with water in a small bowl. Mix well and set aside.

▌ Put sifted glutinous rice flour into a large mixing bowl and make a well in the centre.

▌ Gradually add green tea mixture and combine with flour. Add just enough green tea mixture to form a ball of soft and pliable dough that also does not stick to your palms. Cover and leave to rest for 1 hour.

▌ Slowly knead rested dough and shape into balls the size of kalamansi limes (*limau kesturi*). Place balls on a clean plate and cover with a tea towel to prevent drying.

▌ Prepare filling. Deep-fry peanuts over moderate–low heat until light brown. Drain on paper towels and leave to cool.

▌ Blend (process) cooled peanuts until fine, then mix with sugar. Shape peanut mixture into balls slightly smaller than dough balls. Refrigerate for 10 minutes before use.

▌ To assemble, make a well in a portion of dough and put a portion of peanut filling inside. Seal and reshape into a ball. Repeat until ingredients are used up.

▌ Cook green tea dumplings in a pot of boiling water. When they float to the surface, remove with a slotted spoon and lower into prepared syrup.

▌ Serve warm or at room temperature, garnished with sesame seeds.

Banana Rolls

Grated skinned tapioca (cassava)	400 g (13½ oz)
Tapioca flour	40 g (1¼ oz)
Coconut cream	150 ml (5 fl oz), squeezed from 1 grated coconut
Screwpine (*pandan*) juice	50 ml (1¾ fl oz)
Food colouring of choice (optional)	a drop
Castor (superfine) sugar	150 g (5 oz)
Salt	½ tsp
Banana leaves	3 pieces, each 26 x 20 cm (10½ x 8 in)
Bananas	3, about 250 g (9 oz) with skin intact, preferably *tanduk* variety
Kitchen twine or string for tying	
Grated skinned coconut	100 g (3½ oz), mixed with ½ tsp salt

▌ Combine grated tapioca, tapioca flour, coconut cream, screwpine juice, food colouring, if using, sugar and salt in a steaming bowl. Mix well.

▌ Steam mixture for 5 minutes or until thickened, stirring occasionally. Divide steamed batter into 3 equal portions.

▌ Spread each portion of batter along the centre of a banana leaf and top with a peeled banana. Roll up tightly into a cylindrical shape, then twist both ends to seal and tie with kitchen twine or string to secure.

▌ Steam rolls over high heat for 15–20 minutes or until cooked.

▌ Remove banana leaves from cooled rolls and slice into 2-cm (1-in) pieces.

▌ Roll edges of banana roll pieces in salted grated coconut and serve as a dessert.

Caramel Bananas en Papillote

INGREDIENTS

Bananas	6, just ripened, preferably *raja* variety
Greaseproof paper	4 sheets, each 20 x 20 cm (8 x 8 in)
Ice cream (optional)	

Caramel sauce

Single (light) cream	150 ml (5 fl oz)
Brown sugar	70 g (2 1/2 oz)
Butter	30 g (1 oz)

Chocolate sauce

Single (light) cream	120 ml (4 fl oz)
Dark chocolate	80 g (3 oz), grated
Rum (optional)	2 Tbsp

METHOD

▌ Peel and halve bananas lengthways. Set aside.

▌ Prepare caramel sauce. Combine all ingredients in a bowl, stir to blend and set aside.

▌ Fold each piece of greaseproof paper in half and smooth open again.

▌ Place 3 banana halves on one half of each piece of greaseproof paper, then drizzle caramel sauce over.

▌ Re-fold paper in half to cover bananas. Fold edges of 3 open sides together twice to secure and seal parcel.

▌ With prepared parcels on a baking tray, bake in a preheated oven at 180°C (350°F) for 8–10 minutes, depending on the ripeness of the bananas.

▌ Meanwhile, prepare chocolate sauce. Heat cream in a saucepan and add grated chocolate. Stir until chocolate is melted, then turn off heat and mix in rum, if using. Set aside.

▌ To check bananas for doneness, press lightly through the paper with the back of a fork; the bananas should be quite soft. When done, remove from oven.

▌ To serve, remove bananas from paper parcels and transfer to serving plates. Top with a scoop of ice cream, if you like, and drizzle chocolate sauce over.

▌ Another serving suggestion is to transfer baked parcels directly to serving plates and let diners have the pleasure of opening the parcels themselves, with the chocolate sauce in a serving bowl on the side. Do remind diners to be careful as the steam trapped inside the parcels can be very hot.

Note: En papillote is the French term for baking in paper.

Indonesian Sago Dessert

Multi-coloured sago pearls 100 g (3¹/₂ oz)

Green (mung) bean flour
 (*hoon kwe*)   100 g (3¹/₂ oz)

Coconut milk   500 ml (16 fl oz / 2 cups),
                                squeezed from 1 grated
                                coconut with sufficient water
                                added

Castor (superfine) sugar   120 g (4 oz)

Screwpine (*pandan*)
 leaves   2, washed and knotted

Salt   ¹/₄ tsp

Banana leaves or
 shiny plastic sheets   25, each 19 x 13 cm
                                (7¹/₂ x 5 in)

METHOD

▌ Prepare filling. Bring a pot of water to the boil, add sago pearls and cook, stirring occasionally, for 10 minutes.

▌ Turn off heat, cover pot and let sago sit for another 10 minutes.

▌ Drain sago pearls and rinse under cool tap water until water runs clear. Drain in a colander.

▌ Combine green bean flour and coconut milk in a mixing bowl. Stir to blend, then strain into a clean saucepan.

▌ Add sugar, screwpine leaves and salt. Cook over low heat until mixture thickens, stirring continuously with a whisk. When done, stir in sago pearls.

▌ To assemble, spoon 2 tsp filling onto the centre of each banana leaf or plastic sheet.

▌ Fold into thirds lengthways to enclose filling, then fold down both short ends so the weight of the parcel rests on them. Repeat until ingredients are used up.

▌ Pinch each parcel at the centre and leave to set completely. Serve at room temperature or chilled.

Note: **This Indonesian dessert is also known as** *cantik manis,* **which literally translates into "pretty sweet".**

Sweet Potato Dumplings with Peanut Filling

INGREDIENTS

Orange-fleshed sweet potatoes	200 g (7 oz), steamed until soft and peeled
Glutinous rice flour	250 g (9 oz), sifted
Rice flour	50 g (2 oz), sifted
Hot water	200–220 ml (6$\frac{1}{2}$–7 fl oz)
Cooking oil	120 ml (4 fl oz)
Margarine	1 Tbsp
Banana leaves	30 circular pieces, each 4 cm (2 in) in diameter
Cooking oil for brushing	
Black sesame seeds for garnishing	

Filling

Cooking oil	1 Tbsp
Grated skinned coconut	150 g (5 oz)
Coconut cream	2 Tbsp
Sugar	120 g (4 oz)
Ground peanuts (groundnuts)	120 g (4 oz), toasted
White sesame seeds	1 Tbsp, toasted
Salt	a pinch

METHOD

❚ Prepare filling. Heat oil in a pan. Add grated coconut, coconut cream and sugar. Cook until mixture is glossy and thickened.

❚ Mix in ground peanuts, sesame seeds and salt. Dish out and set aside to cool.

❚ Prepare sweet potato skins. Mash steamed sweet potatoes, then using your fingers, slowly rub in both flours until mixture resembles breadcrumbs.

❚ Add hot water, cooking oil and margarine. Mix with a wooden spoon until combined.

❚ Knead mixture into a smooth and pliable dough. Divide dough into 30 g (1 oz) balls.

❚ With each portion of dough, form a well at the centre and place some filling inside. Bring edges together to seal, then reshape into a ball.

❚ Place each filled sweet potato dumpling onto a greased banana leaf.

❚ Steam dumplings for 8–10 minutes or until cooked.

❚ Brush cooked dumplings with oil and garnish with black sesame seeds. Serve warm or at room temperature.

Fruit and Chocolate Purses

INGREDIENTS

Phyllo (filo) pastry	6 pieces, each 40 x 26 cm (16 x 10½ in)
Butter for brushing	
Icing (confectioner's) sugar for garnishing (optional)	

Chocolate filling

Bittersweet chocolate	90 g (3 oz), chopped
Butter	3 Tbsp
Egg yolk	1
Egg	1

Fruit filling

Water	125 ml (4 fl oz / ½ cup)
Dried apricots	100 g (3½ oz), chopped
Butter	1 Tbsp
Pine nuts	1½ Tbsp
Pistachios	1½ Tbsp, chopped
Almonds	2 Tbsp, chopped

Sauce

Brown sugar (optional)	1 Tbsp
Ground cinnamon	¼ tsp + more for garnishing
Butter	3 Tbsp
Whipping (double/heavy) cream	125 ml (4 fl oz / ½ cup)

METHOD

▌ Prepare chocolate filling. Combine chocolate and butter in a heavy saucepan and cook over low heat, stirring constantly, until melted and smooth.

▌ Remove chocolate mixture from heat and leave to cool until lukewarm, then separately whisk in egg yolk and egg.

▌ Refrigerate chocolate filling until almost firm, about 1½ hours.

▌ Prepare fruit filling. Combine water and apricots in a heavy saucepan. Bring to the boil over medium heat and simmer until apricots are soft and water has evaporated. Stir occasionally, about every 5 minutes.

▌ Add butter and stir until melted, then add remaining nuts. Remove from heat and set aside to cool completely.

▌ Prepare sauce. Combine sugar, if using, and cinnamon in a small saucepan. Heat until golden brown, stirring constantly.

▌ Add butter and stir until melted, then add cream.

▌ Simmer sauce until smooth and slightly thickened, about 4 minutes. Remove from heat and set aside until needed.

▌ To assemble, place 1 piece of phyllo pastry on a clean work surface and brush with butter.

▌ Place another sheet of phyllo pastry over the first and brush with butter again. Quarter phyllo pastry stack.

▌ Place 1 Tbsp fruit filling at the centre of each pastry quarter and top with 1 rounded (heaped) Tbsp cold chocolate filling.

▌ Lift edges of pastry and gather above filling, then twist gently to form a purse.

▌ Brush generously with butter and place on a baking tray lined with parchment paper. Repeat until ingredients are used up.

▌ Bake prepared purses in a preheated oven at 180°C (350°F) for about 15 minutes or until lightly golden.

▌ To serve, sprinkle purses with extra ground cinnamon and icing sugar, if desired, and drizzle warm sauce over.

Note: **Parchment paper is made from silicon, which makes it resistant to grease, moisture and to some degree, heat. Lining a baking tray with parchment paper allows the baked items to be removed with ease and quickly.**

Water Chestnut and Coconut Jelly

Screwpine (*pandan*) leaves	30, each 12.5-cm (5-in) long
Stapler and staples	

Bottom Layer

Water	300 ml (10 fl oz / 1¼ cup)
Screwpine (*pandan*) leaves	4, sliced
Green (mung) bean flour	30 g (1 oz)
Plain (all-purpose) flour	10 g (⅓ oz)
Tapioca (cassava) flour	1 tsp
Green food colouring (optional)	a drop
Sugar	70 g (2½ oz)
Water chestnuts	5, peeled and cubed

Top Layer

Coconut cream	300 ml (10 fl oz / 1¼ cup)
Corn flour (cornstarch)	15 g (½ oz)
Green (mung) bean flour (*hoon kwe*)	1 tsp
Salt	a pinch

METHOD

▌ Prepare screwpine leaf casings. Snip each length of screwpine leaf halfway, from edge to central stem, at 2.5-cm intervals. Fold along the resulting 4 cuts to form a box-like casing, then staple to secure. Set aside.

▌ Prepare bottom layer. Combine water and screwpine leaves in a blender (processor) until fine. Strain for screwpine juice and set aside.

▌ Combine all flours, screwpine juice and food colouring, if using, in a bowl. Mix well, then strain into a small saucepan.

▌ Add sugar and water chestnuts. Cook over low heat, stirring continuously with a whisk, until mixture thickens and turns translucent.

▌ Remove bottom-layer mixture from heat and immediately half-fill screwpine leaf casings with it, then leave to set.

▌ Prepare top layer. Combine all ingredients in a small saucepan. Cook over low heat, stirring continuously with a whisk, until mixture thickens. Remove from heat.

▌ Spoon top-layer mixture over green layer already in screwpine leaf casings.

▌ When done, refrigerate until set. Serve cold.

Note: **This is a favourite Thai dessert known as** *tako*. **When preparing** *tako*, **it is important to use freshly squeezed coconut cream because processed coconut cream, i.e. those in tetra paks, will lead to cracked surfaces when refrigerated.**

Lotus Flowers

Lotus paste (*leen yong*)   300 g (10 oz)

Pink water dough
High gluten (bread) flour   150 g (5 oz)
Vegetable shortening   30 g (1 oz)
Warm water   80 ml (2$\frac{1}{2}$ fl oz)
Pink food colouring   a drop

Green water dough
High gluten (bread) flour   150 g (5 oz)
Vegetable shortening   30 g (1 oz)
Warm water   80 ml (2$\frac{1}{2}$ fl oz)
Green food colouring   a drop

Oil dough
Plain (all-purpose) flour   300 g (10 oz)
Vegetable shortening   160 g (5$\frac{1}{2}$ oz)

METHOD

▌ Prepare pink water dough. Combine flour and shortening in a mixing bowl. Gradually add water and pink food colouring, kneading to obtain a soft dough. Divide into 10 equal portions and set aside.

▌ Prepare green water dough. Repeat steps for pink water dough, but use green food colouring instead. Set aside.

▌ Prepare oil dough. Combine flour and shortening, kneading until a soft dough forms. Divide into 20 equal portions and set aside.

▌ Using a rolling pin, roll out each portion of pink and green dough into a round. Place a ball of oil dough on top of each, then gather up edges to enclose oil dough completely.

▌ Flatten each mixed dough parcel into a round with a rolling pin.

▌ Put some lotus paste filling onto each round of pink dough. Gather up edges of dough and reshape into a ball.

▌ Wrap filled pink dough ball with a round of green dough. Using a sharp knife, slit 8 times crossways over the green skin as shown on pg 144.

▌ Deep-fry prepared lotus flowers over moderate heat for 8 minutes or until the green petals open up.

▌ Remove and drain on absorbent paper towels. Serve.

Note: **This is often served during the Autumn or Mooncake Festival, which falls on the fifteenth day of the eighth month of the Chinese lunar calendar. Ready-made lotus paste can be bought from baking shops and certain supermarkets.**

Durian Rolls

INGREDIENTS

Plain (all-purpose) flour	150 g (5 oz), sifted
Egg	1, large
Milk	150 ml (5 fl oz)
Water	100 ml (3¹/₂ oz)
Salt	¹/₄ tsp
Coconut cream	50 ml (2 oz)
Corn oil	1 Tbsp
Butta vanilla essence (extract) (optional)	1 tsp
Cooking oil for greasing	
Ground cinnamon for dusting	

Chocolate sauce

Bittersweet chocolate	45 g (1¹/₂ oz), chopped
Butter	1¹/₂ Tbsp
Egg yolk	1

Filling

Whipping (heavy/double) cream	100 g (3¹/₂ oz)
Instant custard powder	3 Tbsp
Milk	2 Tbsp
Fresh durian pulp	250 g (9 oz), mashed with fork
Icing (confectioner's) sugar (optional)	1–2 Tbsp, omit if durian flesh is sweet

METHOD

▌ Prepare chocolate sauce. Combine chocolate and butter in a heavy saucepan. Stir over low heat until melted and smooth.

▌ Remove from heat and leave to cool until lukewarm, then whisk in yolk.

▌ Set aside, covered with cling film (plastic wrap), until required.

▌ Prepare filling. Whisk cream using an electric beater on medium speed until firm peaks form.

▌ Separately combine instant custard and milk in a bowl, then gradually stir into beaten cream with durian pulp and sugar to taste. Refrigerate until required.

▌ Prepare crêpes. Combine all ingredients, except oil for greasing and ground cinnamon, in a bowl. Mix with a wire balloon whisk until well blended.

▌ Strain batter and leave to rest for 30 minutes.

▌ Heat a small non-stick pan over low heat and grease with some oil.

▌ Give batter a quick stir and pour 2–3 Tbsp into pan. Immediately swirl pan so that batter covers the base in a thin layer.

▌ Cook until batter has set and begins to brown, then flip over and cook the other side for just a few seconds.

▌ Turn crêpe out onto a clean tea towel and leave to cool before stacking next crêpe on top. Repeat until ingredients are used up.

▌ The batter tends to thicken as you prepare more crêpes, so you might need to thin it down with 1–2 Tbsp water as you go along.

▌ To assemble, carefully spoon 1 rounded (heaped) Tbsp chilled filling along the centre of a crêpe.

▌ Fold lower edge over to cover filling, then fold in left and right sides and roll up.

▌ Serve drizzled with chocolate sauce and a dust of ground cinnamon.

Note: **Butta vanilla is a type of essence that, as the name suggests, smells more buttery than vanilla essence. If unavailable, however, vanilla essence makes a good substitute.**

Teochew Mooncakes

INGREDIENTS
Greaseproof paper

Filling

Candied lemon	100 g (3¹/₂ oz), chopped
Candied winter melon (*tung kwa*)	100 g (3¹/₂ oz), chopped
White sesame seeds	40 g (1¹/₄ oz), toasted
Preserved vegetables (*mui choy*)	50 g (2 oz), soaked, chopped and dry-fried until dry, about 3 minutes
Lotus paste (*leen yong*)	250 g (9 oz)
Cooking oil	1 Tbsp
Cooked glutinous flour (*ko fun*) (optional)	2 Tbsp

Water dough

Vegetable shortening	100 g (3¹/₂ oz)
Sugar	1 Tbsp
Plain (all-purpose) flour	230 g (7¹/₂ oz), sifted
Water	90 ml (3 oz)

Oil dough

Plain (all-purpose) flour	150 g (5 oz), sifted
Vegetable shortening	80 g (3 oz)

METHOD

▎ Prepare filling. Combine all ingredients in a mixing bowl and divide into 10 equal balls. Set aside.

▎ Prepare water dough. Combine and blend shortening and sugar in a bowl. Add plain flour and water. Mix well to form a soft dough.

▎ Knead dough until smooth, then cover with a tea towel and set aside for 30 minutes.

▎ Prepare oil dough. Combine plain flour and shortening to form a soft dough. Divide into 10 equal portions and set aside.

▎ To assemble, shape water dough into a long roll. Cut into 10 equal pieces. Lay each piece on its cut side and use a rolling pin to flatten it into a round large enough to wrap a portion of oil dough.

▎ Put a piece of oil dough on top of each water dough round, then gather up edges to enclose and seal. Repeat until ingredients are used up.

▎ Flatten and roll out each dough parcel on a lightly floured surface into a long rectangular shape. Roll up dough Swiss-roll style.

▎ Flatten log of dough into a rectangle and roll it up again.

▎ Turn the roll onto its side and flatten it a third time into a 15-cm (6-in) round, then place a ball of filling at the centre.

▎ Gather edges of the dough above the filling and twist to seal, enclosing the filling within. Pinch away the extra dough.

▎ Flatten the filled mooncake slightly with your palm.

▎ Prick some holes on the surface of each mooncake and place mooncakes onto a greased tray.

▎ Bake in a preheated oven at 180°C (350°F), turning over once, until they are light brown, about 10 minutes.

▎ When done, remove from oven and leave to cool. Wrap mooncakes in greaseproof paper to store.

Note: Cooked glutinous rice flour is glutinous rice flour that has been dry-fried. Both cooked glutinous rice flour and lotus paste can be bought ready-made at stores selling baking supplies during the period just before the Autumn or Mooncake Festival.

Traditional Kuih

Palm Leaves

Nyonya Lepat Kacang

INGREDIENTS

Black-eyed beans	150 g (5 oz), washed and soaked in water overnight
Glutinous rice	250 g (9 oz), washed and soaked in water overnight
Screwpine (*pandan*) leaves	2, knotted
Coconut cream	150 ml (5 oz), squeezed from $^1/_2$ grated coconut
Salt	1 tsp or to taste
Sugar	6 Tbsp
Grated skinned coconut	100 g (3$^1/_2$ oz)
Unopened *licuala* palm (*palas*) leaves	3 sticks

METHOD

▌ Drain black-eyed beans and place in a small saucepan. Add sufficient water to immerse them completely.

▌ Bring to the boil and cook for 10 minutes or until beans are tender but not mushy. Drain and set aside.

▌ Drain glutinous rice using a colander, then transfer to a medium pot. Add boiled beans, screwpine leaves, coconut cream, salt, sugar and grated coconut.

▌ Cook over medium heat until most of the coconut cream has been absorbed. Stir occasionally to prevent sticking.

▌ Trim off jagged top edges of palm leaves, if desired, then separate into strips about 8-cm (3-in) wide along the leaf's grain.

▌ Fold one end of leaf into a cone as shown on pg 146 and fill with rice mixture.

▌ Finish folding leaf into a triangular parcel and tie a knot to secure. Repeat until ingredients are used up; this recipe makes about 15 parcels.

▌ Bring a large stockpot of water to the boil. Lower in parcels, making sure they are completely immersed, and cook over medium heat for 30–40 minutes or until done.

▌ Add more water and continue boiling if the rice is still hard at the end of cooking time.

▌ Remove and drain cooked parcels. Serve as a snack during tea time.

Note: Add some natural blue food colouring for decorative variation. The blue colouring is obtained by boiling dried clitoria petals (*bunga terlang*) in some water and strained.

Abok-abok Sago

INGREDIENTS

Banana leaves	20 circles, each 22 cm (9 in) in diameter and scalded to soften
Bamboo skewers or cocktail sticks	

Palm sugar filling

Palm sugar (*gula Melaka*)	150 g (5 oz), chopped
Castor (superfine) sugar	2 Tbsp

Sago filling

Sago pearls	200 g (7 oz), soaked in water for 10 minutes and drained
Grated skinned coconut	80 g (3 oz)
Coconut cream	125 ml (4 fl oz / 2^1/$_2$ cup)
Castor (superfine) sugar	4 Tbsp
Salt	^{1}/$_2$ tsp
Thick screwpine (*pandan*) juice	1 Tbsp
Green food colouring (optional)	1 drop

METHOD

▌ Prepare palm sugar filling. Combine both sugars in a bowl and set aside.

▌ Prepare sago filling. Combine pre-soaked sago pearls, grated coconut, coconut cream, sugar and salt in a mixing bowl.

▌ Divide sago mixture into 2 equal portions and add screwpine juice to one. Alternatively, prepare more screwpine juice and colour the entire sago mixture green.

▌ To assemble, fold each banana leaf into a semi-circle, then into a cone as shown on pg 147.

▌ Fill cone halfway with plain sago mixture, then add 1 tsp palm sugar filling. Top with sufficient green sago mixture until it reaches 3 cm (1^1/$_2$ in) from the top.

▌ Fold down rim of banana leaf cone to cover filling and secure with a bamboo skewer or cocktail stick. Repeat until ingredients are used up.

▌ Steam *abok-abok* cones over rapidly boiling water for 12–15 minutes.

▌ Serve, wrapped or unwrapped, at room temperature as a tea-time snack.

Kuih Bongkong

INGREDIENTS

Rice flour	70 g (2½ oz)
Corn flour (cornstarch)	50 g (2 oz)
Tapioca (cassava) flour	30 g (1 oz)
Coconut milk	750 ml (24 fl oz / 3 cups), squeezed from 2 grated coconuts with sufficient water added
Screwpine (*pandan*) leaves	2, knotted
Castor (superfine) sugar	1 Tbsp
Salt	1 tsp
Banana leaves	2, each 20 x 17 cm (8 x 7 in), scalded to soften
Palm sugar (*gula Melaka*)	100 g (3½ oz), chopped
Bamboo skewers or cocktail sticks	

METHOD

▮ Prepare batter. Combine flours and coconut milk in a mixing bowl. Blend with a balloon whisk.

▮ Strain batter into a saucepan. Add screwpine leaves, castor sugar and salt.

▮ Cook over low heat, stirring continuously, until batter thickens. Remove from heat and set aside.

▮ Spoon 1 Tbsp batter onto the centre of a banana leaf. Top with 1 tsp palm sugar, then cover filling with 1 Tbsp batter.

▮ Wrap up as shown on pg 146, then secure parcel with a bamboo skewer or cocktail stick.

▮ Steam parcels over rapidly boiling water for 10 minutes or until cooked.

▮ Remove from heat and leave to cool. Serve *kuih* as a tea-time snack.

Traditional Kuih Lopis

INGREDIENTS

Glutinous rice	600 g (1 lb 5 oz), washed and drained
Screwpine (*pandan*) juice	750 ml (24 fl oz / 3 cups)
Alkaline water (*kan sui*)	1 Tbsp
Salt	1 tsp
Banana leaves	25 strips, 8-cm (9-in) wide
Kitchen twine or string for tying	
Grated skinned coconut	100 g (3 1/2 oz), mixed with 1/2 tsp salt

Syrup

Palm sugar (*gula Melaka*)	250 g (9 oz), chopped
Rock sugar	50 g (2 oz)
Water	250 ml (8 fl oz / 1 cup)
Screwpine (*pandan*) leaves	2, knotted

METHOD

▌ Place glutinous rice, screwpine juice, alkaline water and salt in a saucepan. Cook, stirring frequently, over low heat until liquid has evaporated. The rice is only half-cooked at this stage. Set aside.

▌ Prepare syrup. Combine all ingredients in a saucepan. Bring to the boil and simmer for 8 minutes over low heat. Strain into a clean bowl. Set aside.

▌ Take a banana leaf strip and fold one end into a cone as shown on pg 147. Fill it with glutinous rice.

▌ Continue folding leaf into a triangular parcel as shown, then secure with kitchen string. Repeat until ingredients are used up.

▌ Bring a large pot of water to the boil. Lower in *kuih* and cook for 1 hour. Drain and set aside to cool.

▌ Remove banana leaves from cooled *kuih* and coat *kuih* with salted grated coconut. Drizzle palm sugar syrup over and serve.

Note: **Banana leaf strips have to be prepared or cut along the grain of the leaf, and not against it. Cooks often wind up with strips of varying lengths after trimming away torn or unusable parts. Double or triple wrap the *kuih* to seal completely and prevent leakages during boiling.**

Sweet Potato Kuih Ku

INGREDIENTS

Sweet potatoes	200 g (7 oz), peeled and steamed for 20 minutes or until soft
Castor (superfine) sugar	1 tsp
Glutinous rice flour	250 g (9 oz)
Hot water	100 ml (3½ fl oz)
Cooking oil	120–150 ml (4–5 fl oz / 8–10 Tbsp)
Kuih ku mould (see pg 143)	
Banana leaves	cut into 6-cm (2½-in) squares or circles and brushed with oil
Cooking oil for brushing	

Filling

Skinned green (mung) beans	200 g (7 oz), soaked in water for 1 hour if steaming
Screwpine (*pandan*) leaves	2–3
Castor (superfine) sugar	120 g (4 oz)
Salt	¼ tsp
Cooking oil	90–105 ml (3–3½ fl oz / 6–7 Tbsp)

METHOD

▮ Prepare filling. Pressure-cook green beans and screwpine leaves for 10 minutes. Alternatively, steam pre-soaked green beans for 20 minutes or until soft. Discard screwpine leaves.

▮ Combine green beans, sugar, salt and oil in a blender (processor) until a smooth paste results.

▮ Shape paste into balls the size of limes (*limau nipis*) and set aside.

▮ Prepare *kuih* skin. Mash steamed sweet potatoes with sugar, then gradually mix in glutinous rice flour until mixture resembles breadcrumbs.

▮ Add hot water and oil, mixing with a spatula until a soft dough forms.

▮ Divide dough into balls large enough to snugly fit into the *kuih ku* mould.

▮ To assemble, first form a well in each portion of dough. Place a ball of filling inside, then wrap dough around it and reseal.

▮ If dough is a little sticky, lightly dust the mould with some glutinous rice flour before pressing in the filled dough.

▮ Knock mould gently against the work surface to dislodge the *kuih* and turn it out onto a piece of greased banana leaf. Repeat until ingredients are used up.

▮ Steam prepared *kuih* over medium heat for 8–10 minutes.

▮ Lightly grease cooked *kuih* with some oil and serve.

Note: Use orange-fleshed sweet potatoes for orange *kuih ku* skins and, correspondingly, purple-fleshed sweet potatoes for purple skins.

Kuih Kochi

Sugar	50 g (2 oz)
Water	30 ml (1 oz)
Screwpine (*pandan*) leaves	2, knotted
Skinned grated coconut	100 g (3¹/₂ oz)
Salt	a pinch
Coconut cream	2 Tbsp
Corn flour (cornstarch)	1 tsp
Toasted sesame seeds	¹/₂ Tbsp
Banana leaves	20 circles, each 22 cm (9 in) in diameter, greased

Skin

Glutinous rice flour	150 g (5 oz)
Tapioca (cassava) flour	60 g (2 oz)
Salt	a pinch
Coconut cream	200–220 ml (6¹/₂–7¹/₂ oz), squeezed from ¹/₂ coconut
Natural blue food colouring (optional)	1 tsp

METHOD

- Prepare filling. Combine sugar, water and screwpine leaves in a small saucepan over medium heat. Cook until sugar is dissolved.

- Add grated coconut and salt. Continue cooking, stirring well, until it is thick and glossy, about 8 minutes.

- Combine coconut cream and corn flour, then add to coconut mixture. Turn off heat and stir in sesame seeds.

- When filling is cool enough to handle, shape into balls the size of limes (*limau nipis*). Set aside.

- Prepare *kuih* skin. Combine flours and salt in a mixing bowl.

- Blend in sufficient coconut cream to form a smooth, pliable dough. Knead well.

- Measure up and separate 100 g (3¹/₂ oz) dough. Mix in blue colouring, then set both white and blue doughs aside for 30 minutes, covered with a damp tea towel.

- To assemble *kuih*, combine a bit of blue dough with some white dough to form a 3.5-cm (1¹/₂-in) ball; do not knead to blend. Repeat until ingredients are used up.

- Using fingers, form a well at the centre of each dough ball. Put a portion of coconut filling inside and gather up edges of dough to enclose and seal.

- Fold a greased banana leaf into a cone and place filled dough inside. The method of folding here is similar to that for *abok-abok sago* on pg 147.

- Fold in rim of banana leaf cone to enclose filled dough and secure. Repeat until ingredients are used up.

- Arrange *kuih koci* cones in a single layer on a steaming tray and steam over rapidly boiling water for 10 minutes.

- Remove from heat and leave to cool. Serve at room temperature.

Lepat Pisang

INGREDIENTS

Coconut milk	375 ml (12 fl oz / 1½ cups), squeezed from 1 coconut with sufficient water added
Rice flour	35 g (1 oz)
Corn flour (cornstarch)	25 g (1 oz)
Tapioca (cassava) flour	1 Tbsp
Salt	1 tsp or to taste
Sugar	1 Tbsp
Banana leaves	10 pieces, each 20 x 12.5 cm (8 x 5 in), scalded to soften
Fresh bananas	5, peeled and sliced horizontally, preferably *raja* variety
Bamboo skewers or cocktail sticks	

METHOD

▮ In a bowl, whisk together coconut milk and all the flours.

▮ Strain flour mixture into a small saucepan, then add salt and sugar. Cook over low heat, stirring continuously, until mixture thickens. Remove from heat.

▮ Place 2 Tbsp batter at the centre of a banana leaf and top with a slice of banana.

▮ Fold banana leaf into thirds lengthways as shown on pg 146 for *pulut inti*, only fold up the short ends instead of down and secure with bamboo skewers or cocktail sticks.

▮ Trim off any excess leaf. Repeat until ingredients are used up.

▮ Arrange parcels in a single layer on a steaming tray and steam over rapidly boiling water for 10 minutes or until cooked.

▮ Remove from steamer and serve warm or at room temperature.

Note: Traditionally, each banana leaf was folded into thirds lengthways to completely enclose the filling, and the short ends would be folded down so that the weight of the parcel rests on them.

Pulut Inti

Glutinous rice	250 g (9 oz), washed and soaked in water overnight
Screwpine (*pandan*) leaves	2, knotted
Pure coconut cream (*pati santan*)	150 ml (5 fl oz), squeezed from 1/2 grated coconut
Salt	1 tsp or to taste
Sugar	2 Tbsp
Natural blue food colouring (optional)	
Banana leaves	10 pieces, each 14 x 12 cm (5 1/2 x 5 in), scalded to soften

Coconut filling

Palm sugar (*gula Melaka*)	200 g (7 oz)
Water	150 ml (5 fl oz)
Screwpine (*pandan*) leaves	2, knotted
Grated skinned coconut	250 g (9 oz)
Salt	1/2 tsp

METHOD

▐ Prepare coconut filling. Combine palm sugar, water and screwpine leaves in a small saucepan. Cook over low heat until sugar dissolves.

▐ Remove from heat and strain mixture into a clean saucepan.

▐ Stir in grated coconut and salt. Place mixture over the heat again and continue cooking, stirring well, until mixture is thick and glossy, about 10 minutes.

▐ Remove from heat and set aside to cool.

▐ Meanwhile, prepare rice. Drain glutinous rice in a colander and transfer to a steaming tray with screwpine leaves. Steam over rapidly boiling water for 15–20 minutes.

▐ Combine coconut cream, salt and sugar in a bowl. Stir until dissolved.

▐ Pour coconut cream over hot, steamed glutinous rice. Set aside until coconut cream is absorbed.

▐ If using blue food colouring, divide prepared glutinous rice into 2 equal portions and add it to one.

▐ To assemble, spoon 1 Tbsp rice, mixing plain and blue if applicable, onto the centre of a banana leaf. Top with 1 tsp coconut filling, then fold as shown on pg 146.

▐ Serve as a tea-time snack.

Note: If available, the dried petals of clitoria flowers or *bunga terlang* may be boiled in some water to obtain a natural blue food colouring.

Onde-onde

Sweet potatoes	125 g (4¹/₂ oz), peeled and steamed until soft
Glutinous rice flour	200 g (7 oz)
Coconut milk	150 ml (5 fl oz), squeezed from ¹/₂ grated coconut with sufficient water added
Thick screwpine (*pandan*) juice	2 Tbsp
Green food colouring (optional)	a drop
Palm sugar (*gula Melaka*)	100 g (3¹/₂ oz), chopped or grated
Grated skinned coconut	100 g (3¹/₂ oz), mixed with ¹/₂ tsp salt
Toasted white sesame seeds for garnishing	

METHOD

▌ Prepare *kuih* skin. Remove tough fibres in sweet potatoes, then mash until fine in a mixing bowl.

▌ Mix in glutinous rice flour. Slowly add in sufficient coconut milk and screwpine juice to form a dough. Add green food colouring, if using.

▌ Measure up 50 g dough and steam over high heat for 5 minutes. This is known to some as *ibu*, or "mother", dough.

▌ Remove *ibu* dough from steamer and knead it into the uncooked dough. Knead until resulting dough is soft and pliable. Add more screwpine juice, if necessary.

▌ Leave dough to rest, covered with a tea towel, for ¹/₂–1 hour. If rested dough is too soft, mix in a little extra glutinous rice flour.

▌ Bring a pot of water to the boil.

▌ Pinch out enough dough to form a ball the size of a kalamansi lime (*limau kesturi*) and make a well at the centre.

▌ Fill with ¹/₂ tsp palm sugar and gather up edges of dough to enclose the sugar and reshape into a ball.

▌ Immediately lower filled *onde-onde* into rapidly boiling water and cook until it floats to the surface. Remove with a slotted spoon.

▌ Allow cooked *onde-onde* to drain a while before rolling in grated coconut, then set aside. Repeat until ingredients are used up.

▌ Serve at room temperature and sprinkled with sesame seeds.

Note: Ibu means "mother" in Malay and *onde-onde* is a popular, traditional Malay snack. Traditional preparation of *onde-onde* involved reshaping the filled dough into a tear-drop shape through pinching. This method, however, requires much time and skill. The tear-drop shape makes the skin considerably thinner and, thus, more enjoyable for the diner, but the thinner skin is also more prone to tears and ruptures during cooking.

Wrapping Techniques

Vegetables

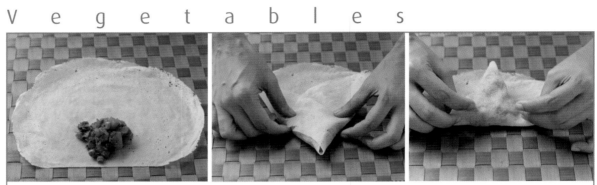

1. To wrap a samosa, measure 3 cm from the edge of *popiah* skin and cut across in a straight line. Spoon 1 rounded (heaped) Tbsp filling near the centre of the cut edge.
2. Take one end of cut edge and fold over the filling. Repeat with other end to form a triangular tip and secure with flour paste.
3. Fold triangular parcel over (as shown), then dab flour paste along circular edge. Fold up left and right sides to seal.

Sweets

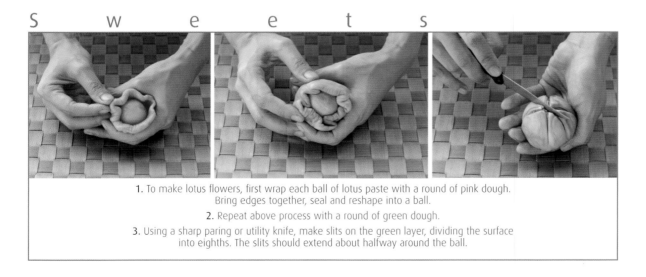

1. To make lotus flowers, first wrap each ball of lotus paste with a round of pink dough. Bring edges together, seal and reshape into a ball.
2. Repeat above process with a round of green dough.
3. Using a sharp paring or utility knife, make slits on the green layer, dividing the surface into eighths. The slits should extend about halfway around the ball.

1. Overlap two bamboo leaves lengthways, with their stems at opposite ends. Spoon filling onto the centre, then fold in both long sides to enclose filling.

2. Ensure that filling is totally enclosed before folding in left and right sides, one on top of the other.

3. Tie parcel with pre-soaked hemp string to secure. To tie, wind hemp along the length of the parcel first, then across several times.

1. Trim off hard ends of each cabbage leaf before arranging as shown—in a tripod fashion, with the leafy ends overlapping in the bowl.

2. After spooning in basil rice, fold in ends of cabbage leaves to enclose rice, one on top of the other.

3. To serve, take a serving plate and cover the bowl before turning over. Lift bowl when ready to serve.

1. Begin by overlapping two bamboo leaves lengthways, with their stems at opposite ends.

2. Fold leaves to form a cone at the centre. Check that there is no 'hole' at the bottom before adding rice and filling.

3. Once filled, lightly pinch either side of the cone (as shown) before firmly folding down bamboo leaves to cover ingredients. Continue to fold along the cone until a pyramid shape forms.

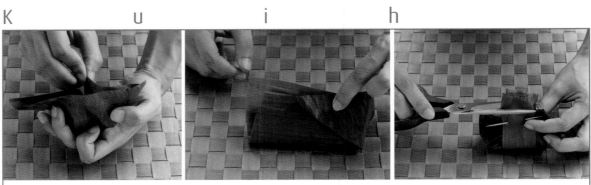

1. To wrap *kuih bongkong*, bring two long sides together after adding filling, then push one edge up (as shown), so two triangular flaps form on either side.

2. Fold both triangular flaps in towards the centre, then repeat with other end.

3. Take a strip of banana leaf and wrap around the centre of the parcel. Secure with a bamboo skewer or cocktail stick. Lastly, trim off excess leaf.

1. To wrap *pulut inti*, first fold one long edge of banana leaf over to partially cover ingredients. Secure position of leaf by pressing down with thumbs at either end of the rice filling.

2. With thumbs holding the first folded edge in place, lift and fold over the other long edge in the same way.

3. Fold both ends under so the weight of the parcel rests on them.

1. To wrap *lepat kacang*, unfurl the non-stem end of palm leaf and fold into a cone.

2. After filling cone, fold down excess leaf to cover ingredients and tuck stem end, which has been left intact, through the opening in the cone.

3. Tie a knot with the unfurled parts of the leaf to secure parcel.

1. For *abok-abok* sago cones, first fold banana leaf circle in half, then twist semi-circle into a cone. Note that the twisting hand should be inside the fold, where the filling would be added later.

2. Once filled, fold down one side of the rim to cover ingredients, then fold in left and right sides. Fold down the last section and secure with a bamboo skewer or cocktail stick.

3. Once secured, turn cone over and repeat with remaining ingredients until used up.

1. To wrap *kuih lopis*, take a banana leaf strip and fold one end upwards to form a cone.

2. After adding filling, fold excess leaf over to cover ingredients, then continue to fold along the triangular parcel until leaf is used up.

3. Take a second banana leaf strip and double wrap the parcel. Inspect parcel and assess if it needs to be wrapped a third time to prevent leakage. Secure parcel with hemp or raffia.

Weights and Measures

Quantities for this book are given in Metric, Imperial and American (spoon and cup) measures. Standard spoon and cup measurements used are: 1 tsp = 5 ml, 1 Tbsp = 15 ml, 1 cup = 250 ml. All measures are level unless otherwise stated.

LIQUID AND VOLUME MEASURES

Metric	Imperial	American
5 ml	$^1/_6$ fl oz	1 teaspoon
10 ml	$^1/_3$ fl oz	1 dessertspoon
15 ml	$^1/_2$ fl oz	1 tablespoon
60 ml	2 fl oz	$^1/_4$ cup (4 tablespoons)
85 ml	$2^1/_2$ fl oz	$^1/_3$ cup
90 ml	3 fl oz	$^3/_8$ cup (6 tablespoons)
125 ml	4 fl oz	$^1/_2$ cup
180 ml	6 fl oz	$^3/_4$ cup
250 ml	8 fl oz	1 cup
300 ml	10 fl oz ($^1/_2$ pint)	$1^1/_4$ cups
375 ml	12 fl oz	$1^1/_2$ cups
435 ml	14 fl oz	$1^3/_4$ cups
500 ml	16 fl oz	2 cups
625 ml	20 fl oz (1 pint)	$2^1/_2$ cups
750 ml	24 fl oz ($1^1/_5$ pints)	3 cups
1 litre	32 fl oz ($1^3/_5$ pints)	4 cups
1.25 litres	40 fl oz (2 pints)	5 cups
1.5 litres	48 fl oz ($2^2/_5$ pints)	6 cups
2.5 litres	80 fl oz (4 pints)	10 cups

DRY MEASURES

Metric	Imperial
30 grams	1 ounce
45 grams	$1^1/_2$ ounces
55 grams	2 ounces
70 grams	$2^1/_2$ ounces
85 grams	3 ounces
100 grams	$3^1/_2$ ounces
110 grams	4 ounces
125 grams	$4^1/_2$ ounces
140 grams	5 ounces
280 grams	10 ounces
450 grams	16 ounces (1 pound)
500 grams	1 pound, $1^1/_2$ ounces
700 grams	$1^1/_2$ pounds
800 grams	$1^3/_4$ pounds
1 kilogram	2 pounds, 3 ounces
1.5 kilograms	3 pounds, $4^1/_2$ ounces
2 kilograms	4 pounds, 6 ounces

LENGTH

Metric	Imperial
0.5 cm	$^1/_4$ inch
1 cm	$^1/_2$ inch
1.5 cm	$^3/_4$ inch
2.5 cm	1 inch

OVEN TEMPERATURE

	°C	°F	Gas Regulo
Very slow	120	250	1
Slow	150	300	2
Moderately slow	160	325	3
Moderate	180	350	4
Moderately hot	190/200	370/400	5/6
Hot	210/220	410/440	6/7
Very hot	230	450	8
Super hot	250/290	475/550	9/10

ABBREVIATION

tsp	teaspoon
Tbsp	tablespoon
g	gram
kg	kilogram
ml	millilitre